MW00785093

"Robert Klitgaard makes a tantalizi⌐
doors shut tight by muck, offering fresh ideas about how to ...
well and fully. Starting with Annie Dillard's wonderful reflection
on the rich diversity behind assumed values, Klitgaard guides us
through an array of intellectual, moral, and spiritual challenges,
some engaging and some tough, that are bound to set minds and
hearts in motion."

—KATHERINE MARSHALL, executive director, World Faiths Development Dialogue

"Many young people feel there is an incompatibility between faith
and reason, and so they must choose between the two. In *Christianity for Young Intellectuals*, Robert Klitgaard masterfully shreds this
notion, showing that religion and the intellect not only can co-exist;
they are incomplete without each other."

—ARTHUR C. BROOKS, professor of the practice of public leadership, Harvard University

"In this readable and rewarding collection, Robert Klitgaard gathers
diverse thinkers—historians, philosophers, artists, scientists—to
answer the most demanding questions of human experience through
serious engagement with the Christian religion. The essays collected
here are not apologetics in any flat or formal sense. Rather, they
are serious and critical reflections that recognize Christianity as a
complex, living, inspiring, and sometimes troubling tradition, and
which persuasively invite their reader to do the same."

—MATTHEW ICHIHASHI POTTS, professor of Christian morals, Harvard Divinity School

"Are you young, smart, successful in much that you do and yet have a
deep sense that your education, vocation, and relationships still leave
a void? If so, then *Christianity for Young Intellectuals* is a quick yet
profound investigation by some of the world's great intellectuals, who
found hope in looking deeper into this peace-filled story of Jesus."

—JACK JACKSON, president, Foundation for Evangelism

"This book is a must-read for anyone curious about the deeper questions of science, philosophy, and faith. A call to action for young thinkers to re-examine their beliefs."

—ZACHARY SWANSON, PhD student in applied positive psychology, Claremont Graduate University

"*Christianity for Young Intellectuals* took me aback. Much of what passes for apologetic material these days is clear and straight-forward but bland and two-dimensional. The essays in this book, however, expand the apologetic to include voices critical of the faith and others that suggest a literary, artistic approach to faith. The final essay, written by Paul Kingsnorth, is worth the price of admission. I challenge the reader to hold off reading it until the end of the book."

—RICK MATTSON, evangelist/apologist, InterVarsity

"I had a wonderful time reading this much-needed book for Christian intellectuals. It's also perfect for intellectuals, young or old, who are attracted to Christianity, but have stopped short of crossing the threshold of faith."

—GEORGE VARGHESE, distinguished professor of networking, UCLA Computer Science

"The faith taught to us as children will not satisfy us as adults. The faith simplified for mass consumption will not survive the scrutiny of a young intellectual's probing mind. *Christianity for Young Intellectuals* is the challenge, provocation, and practicality that you didn't find in Sunday school classes, preacher sermons, and won't find in Christianity as it's presented by mass media. This book arms young thinkers with a starting point to serious treatment of Christianity's claims, living concepts, and impact on the world. These are exercises for a nuanced, adult engagement with one of history's most influential belief systems."

—MICHAEL MUTHUKRISHNA, author of *A Theory of Everyone*

"The great Wordsworth wrote of Imagination as Reason 'in her most exalted mood.' Robert Klitgaard's judicious and sagacious collection and commentary of texts fires the imagination and challenges the intellect. There is much to reflect upon in these pages: perfect for an inquiring spirit of any age!"

—DOUGLAS HEDLEY, professor of the philosophy of religion, University of Cambridge

Christianity for
Young Intellectuals

Christianity for
Young Intellectuals

Warm-up Exercises for Big Thinkers

EDITED BY

ROBERT KLITGAARD

WIPF & STOCK · Eugene, Oregon

CHRISTIANITY FOR YOUNG INTELLECTUALS
Warm-up Exercises for Big Thinkers

Wipf & Stock
An Imprint of Wipf and Stock Publishers
199 W. 8th Ave., Suite 3
Eugene, OR 97401

www.wipfandstock.com

PAPERBACK ISBN: 979-8-3852-2202-5
HARDCOVER ISBN: 979-8-3852-2203-2
EBOOK ISBN: 979-8-3852-2204-9

08/09/24

To Jesus Estanslao, the epitome of a perennially young intellectual.
You have transformed countless lives, including mine,
and have made the world a better place.

Contents

CONTENTS

PART II | INTRODUCING JESUS

Permissions

Chapter 1. "This Is the Life," by Annie Dillard. Reproduced by permission from Russell & Volkening as agents for Annie Dillard.

Chapter 2. "Real Presences: Two Scientists' Response to George Steiner," by Wilson Poon and Tom McLeish. Reproduced by permission from the authors.

Chapter 3. "A Letter" and "The Universal Grid of Philosophy," by Roberto Mangabeira Unger. Reproduced by permission from the author.

Chapter 4. "Is Life Worth Living?" by William James, Project Gutenberg e-book, public domain. https://www.gutenberg.org/cache/epub/26659/pg26659-images.html

Chapter 5. "Hermits, Addicts, and Heroes," by Robert Klitgaard, open access, reproduced by permission from the author; and excerpts from *Prevail: How to Face Upheavals and Make Big Choices with the Help of Heroes* by Robert Klitgaard, reproduced by permission from Wipf and Stock.

Chapter 6. "What Did Jesus Do?" by Adam Gopnik. Reproduced by permission from The Wylie Agency LLC.

Chapter 7. "War, Peace, and a Crisis in the Life of God," by Jack Miles with an edit by him for this book, and "Crucifixion and the Conscience of the West" by Jack Miles, reproduced by permission from the author.

Chapter 8 "Jesus Christ—Prophet and Reformer," by Leszek Kołakowski. English translation copyright © Agnieszka Kołakowska. Reproduced by permission from Mohrbooks AG Literary Agency as agents for Agnieszka Kołakowska.

Chapter 9. "The Cross and the Machine," by Paul Kingsworth. Reproduced by permission from *First Things*.

List of Contributors

ANNIE DILLARD is an author and novelist. https://www.anniedillard.com

ADAM GOPNIK is a staff writer for *The New Yorker*. https://www.adamgopnik.com

WILLIAM JAMES (1842–1910) was a professor at Harvard University, where he founded the Department of Psychology. https://psychology.fas.harvard.edu/people/william-james

PAUL KINGSNORTH is a poet and novelist. https://www.paulkingsnorth.net

ROBERT KLITGAARD is a University Professor at Claremont Graduate University. https://robertklitgaard.com

LESZEK KOŁAKOWSKI (1927–2009) was a philosopher and historian of ideas who taught at McGill, Chicago, Yale, and Oxford. https://www.newstatesman.com/ideas/2023/06/settling-scores-god-leszek-kolakowski-end-of-history-poland

TOM MCLEISH (1962–2023), a theoretical physicist, was the Chair of Natural Philosophy at the University of York. https://www.york.ac.uk/physics-engineering-technology/about/news/2023/obituary-tom-mcleish/

JACK MILES is Distinguished Professor Emeritus of English & Religious Studies at the University of California, Irvine. https://www.jackmiles.com

WILSON POON is the Chair in Natural Philosophy at the University of Edinburgh and founder of the Edinburgh Complex Fluids Partnership. https://www2.ph.ed.ac.uk/~wckp/

ROBERTO MANGABEIRA UNGER is the Roscoe Pound Professor of Law at Harvard Law School. https://www.robertounger.com

Introduction

IF YOU'RE LIKE MANY young intellectuals, Christianity seems quaint at best. Maybe superstitious. Maybe even pernicious, a sign of an anti-intellectual worldview. You may recognize Paul Kingsnorth's description of our times:

> The age taught another faith: Religion was irrelevant. It was authoritarian, it was superstitious, it was feeble proto-science. It was the theft of our precious free will by authorities who wanted to control us by telling us fairy tales. It repressed women, gay people, atheists, anyone who disobeyed its irrational edicts. It hated science, denied reason, burned witches and heretics by the million. Post-Enlightenment liberal societies had thrown off its shackles, and however hard both species of vicar tried to prevent it, religion was dying a much-needed death at the hands of progress and reason.[1]

Many leading universities downplay, even disdain, the study of religion. For example, a faculty committee at Harvard proposed that every undergraduate should take a course in the category of "Reason and Faith." The idea was defeated. One leading professor said that requiring students to take such a course would be like requiring them to take a course in Astronomy and Astrology. "Faith," he declared, "is believing in something without good reasons to do so. It has no place in anything but a religious institution, and our society has no shortage of these." Peter Gomes—the minister of Harvard's Memorial Church and Plummer Professor of Christian Morals—lamented this "fear that taking religion seriously would undermine everything a great university stands for. I think that's ungrounded, but there it is."[2]

---

1. Kingsnorth, "Cross and Machine," this vol., 153.
2. Miller, "Why Harvard Students," para. 9.

So, if you're like many young intellectuals, your only exposure to Christianity may have been a TV preacher, a random church service, or an off-putting tract.

No wonder the doors of your mind and heart may have shut prematurely.

If so, this book may blow those doors wide open.

Here you'll encounter intriguing thinkers, off-the-radar pieces, and exquisite writing—after all, Annie Dillard (Pulitzer Prize), Adam Gopnik (three National Magazine Awards), Paul Kingsnorth (the Wenlock Prize for poetry and the Gordon Burn Prize for a novel), Robert Klitgaard (a *New York Times* Book of the Century), and Jack Miles (Pulitzer Prize) are celebrated authors. In his day William James was renowned as a speaker and writer, as well as a scientist and philosopher. You'll also encounter two eminent physicists (Wilson Poon and Tom McLeish) and two of the leading philosophers of the past hundred years (Leszek Kołakowski and Roberto Mangabeira Unger).

The first part of the book addresses big questions you may not have verbalized, but once they're raised, they resonate.

Such as, what if you figured out everything—then what?

Where do science and the humanities stop short?

Why is philosophy so impractical?

Is life worth living? Or rather, if it is, what makes it so?

The second part of the book introduces Jesus. You learn why Jesus is uncanny and unique, about his beautiful, horrifying story and his deep—if often unacknowledged by secular thinkers—influence on Western philosophy. The final chapter describes how someone you will admire—a renowned writer, anti-globalization activist, and youthful derider of religion—became . . . a Christian.

But the purpose of these "warm-up exercises for big thinkers" isn't to get you to say amen. It's to scrape away the muck that much secular education has left in place about Christianity. Taking Jesus seriously is often seen as, well, anti-intellectual.

This book promises a different experience. You're invited to join some of the world's most fascinating minds as they challenge misconceptions and illuminate Christianity's profound role in shaping our intellect and imagination. Ready to see the world anew? Let's begin.

PART I

POSING BIG QUESTIONS

1

What If You Could Figure Out Everything? Then What?

As a girl Annie Dillard brimmed with passions from science to baseball, from literature to boys with fast cars. In her twenties, she took off into the woods and wrote a book that ended up winning the Pulitzer Prize (*Pilgrim at Tinker Creek*).

When she was forty, she asked herself what connected the precocious girl, the passionate young woman, and the person she then was.

> Where have they gone, those other dim dots that were you: you in the flesh swimming in a swift river, swinging a bat on the first pitch, opening a footlocker with a screwdriver, inking and painting clowns on celluloid, stepping out of a revolving door into the swift crowd on a sidewalk, being kissed and kissing till your brain grew smooth, stepping out of the cold woods into a warm field full of crows, or lying awake in a bed aware of your legs and suddenly aware of all of it, that the ceiling above you was under the sky—in what country, what town?
>
> You may wonder, that is, as I sometimes wonder privately, but it doesn't matter. For it is not you or I that is important, neither what sort we might be nor how we came to be each where we are. What is important is anyone's coming awake and discovering a place, finding in full orbit a spinning globe one can lean over, catch, and jump on. What is important is the moment of opening a life and feeling it touch—with an electric hiss and cry—this speckled mineral sphere, our present world. . . . I am here now, with this my

own dear family, up here at this high latitude, out here at the far-
thest exploratory tip of this my present bewildering age. And still I
break up through the skin of awareness a thousand times a day, as
dolphins burst through the seas, and dive again, and rise, and dive.[1]

This diving metaphor also occurs in her book *Holy the Firm*—now
describing a God in whom one might have faith.

> Faith would be that God is self-limited utterly by his creation—a
> contraction of the scope of his will; that he bound himself to time
> and its hazards and haps as a man would lash himself to a tree for
> love. That God's works are as good as we make them. That God is
> helpless, our baby to bear, self-abandoned on the doorstep of time,
> wondered at by cattle and oxen. Faith would be that God moved
> and moves once and for all and "down," so to speak, like a diver,
> like a man who eternally gathers himself for a dive and eternally is
> diving, and eternally splitting the spread of the water, and eternally
> drowned."[2]

After the terrorist bombings of September 11, 2001, the editors of a
then-obscure journal invited Dillard and others to reflect on life's meanings. The essay below was her contribution.

You might read it first by yourself, and then read it aloud in a group
with each person taking a paragraph and passing the baton.

DISCUSSION QUESTIONS

1. Reflect on your own intellectual aspirations. Think big. Share some of
   your dreamy intellectual goals.

2. Imagine you were to succeed in knowing what you long to know. Ask
   yourself these questions of Dillard's:

   > What would you do differently, you up on your beanstalk looking
   > at scenes of all peoples at all times in all places? . . .
   >   Say you have seen something. You have seen an ordinary bit of
   > what is real, the infinite fabric of time that eternity shoots through,
   > and time's soft-skinned people working and dying under slowly
   > shifting stars. Then what?[3]

1. Dillard, *American Childhood*, 248–49, 250.
2. Dillard, *Holy the Firm*, 47.
3. Dillard, "This Is the Life," this vol., 7, 8.

This Is the Life

ANNIE DILLARD

Any culture tells you how to live your one and only life: to wit as everyone else does. Probably most cultures prize, as ours rightly does, making a contribution by working hard at work that you love; being in the know, and intelligent; gathering a surplus; and loving your family above all, and your dog, your boat, bird-watching. Beyond those things our culture might specialize in money, and celebrity, and natural beauty. These are not universal. You enjoy work and will love your grandchildren, and somewhere in there you die.

Another contemporary consensus might be: You wear the best shoes you can afford, you seek to know Rome's best restaurants and their staffs, drive the best car, and vacation on Tenerife. And what a cook you are!

Or you take the next tribe's pigs in thrilling raids; you grill yams; you trade for televisions and hunt white-plumed birds. Everyone you know agrees: this is the life. Perhaps you burn captives. You set fire to a drunk. Yours is the human struggle, or the elite one, to achieve . . . whatever your own culture tells you: to publish the paper that proves the point; to progress in the firm and gain high title and salary, stock options, benefits; to get the loan to store the beans till their price rises; to elude capture; to feed your children or educate them to a feather edge; or to count coup or perfect your calligraphy; to eat the king's deer or catch the poacher; to spear the seal, intimidate the enemy, and be a big man or beloved woman and die respected for the pigs or the title or the shoes. Not a funeral. Forget funeral. A big birthday party. Since everyone around you agrees.

Since everyone around you agrees ever since there were people on earth that land is value, or labor is value, or learning is value, or title, necklaces, degree, murex shells, or ownership of slaves. Everyone knows bees sting and ghosts haunt and giving your robes away humiliates your rivals. That the enemies are barbarians. That wise men swim through the rock of the earth; that houses breed filth, airstrips attract airplanes, tornadoes punish, ancestors watch, and you can buy a shorter stay in purgatory. The black rock is holy, or the scroll; or the pangolin is holy, the quetzal is holy, this tree, water, rock, stone, cow, cross, or mountain and it's all true. The Red Sox. Or nothing at all is holy, as everyone intelligent knows.

Who is your "everyone"? Chess masters scarcely surround themselves with motocross racers. Do you want aborigines at your birthday party? Or are you serving yak-butter tea? Popular culture deals not in its distant past, or any other past, or any other culture. You know no one who longs to buy a mule or be named to court or thrown into a volcano.

So the illusion, like the visual field, is complete. It has no holes except books you read and soon forget. And death takes us by storm. What was that, that life? What else offered? If for him it was contract bridge, if for her it was copyright law, if for everyone it was and is an optimal mix of family and friends, learning, contribution, and joy of making and ameliorating, what else is there, or was there, or will there ever be?

What else is a vision or fact of time and the peoples it bears issuing from the mouth of the cosmos, from the round mouth of eternity, in a wide and parti-colored utterance. In the complex weave of this utterance like fabric, in its infinite domestic interstices, the centuries and continents and classes dwell. Each people knows only its own squares in the weave, its wars and instruments and arts, and also the starry sky.

Okay, and then what? Say you scale your own weft and see time's breadth and the length of space. You see the way the fabric both passes among the stars and encloses them. You see in the weave nearby, and aslant farther off, the peoples variously scandalized or exalted in their squares. They work on their projects; they flake spear points, hoe, plant; they kill aurochs or one another; they prepare sacrifices as we here and now work on our projects. What, seeing this spread multiply infinitely in every direction, would you do differently? No one could love your children more; would you love them less? Would you change your project? To what? Whatever you do, it has likely brought delight to fewer people than either contract bridge or the Red Sox.

However hypnotized you and your people are, you will be just as dead in their war, our war. However dead you are, more people will come. However many more people come, your time and its passions, and yourself and your passions, weigh equally in the balance with those of any dead who pulled waterwheel poles by the Nile or Yellow rivers, or painted their foreheads black, or starved in the wilderness, or wasted from disease then or now. Our lives and our deaths count equally, or we must abandon one-man-one-vote, dismantle democracy, and assign six billion people an importance-of-life ranking from one to six billion, a ranking whose number decreases, like gravity, with the square of the distance between us and them.

What would you do differently, you up on your beanstalk looking at scenes of all peoples at all times in all places? When you climb down, would you dance any less to the music you love, knowing that music to be as provisional as a bug? Somebody has to make jugs and shoes, to turn the soil, fish. If you descend the long rope-ladders back to your people and time in the fabric, if you tell them what you have seen, and even if someone cares to listen, then what? Everyone knows times and cultures are plural. If you come back a shrugging relativist or tongue-tied absolutist, then what? If you spend hours a day looking around, high astraddle the warp or woof of your people's wall, then what new wisdom can you take to your grave for worms to untangle? Well, maybe you will not go into advertising.

Then you would know your own death better but perhaps not dread it less. Try to bring people up the wall, carry children to see it to what end? Fewer golf courses? What is wrong with golf? Nothing at all. Equality of wealth? Sure; how?

The woman watching sheep over there, the man who carries embers in a pierced clay ball, the engineer, the girl who spins wool into yarn as she climbs, the smelter, the babies learning to recognize speech in their own languages, the man whipping a slave's flayed back, the man digging roots, the woman digging roots, the child digging roots: what would you tell them? And the future people what are they doing? What excitements sweep peoples here and there from time to time? Into the muddy river they go, into the trenches, into the caves, into the mines, into the granary, into the sea in boats. Most humans who were ever alive lived inside one single culture that never changed for hundreds of thousands of years; archaeologists scratch their heads at so conservative and static a culture.

Over here, the rains fail; they are starving. There, the caribou fail; they are starving. Corrupt leaders take the wealth. Not only there but here. Rust and smut spoil the rye. When pigs and cattle starve or freeze, people die soon after. Disease empties a sector, a billion sectors.

People look at the sky and at the other animals. They make beautiful objects, beautiful sounds, beautiful motions of their bodies beating drums in lines. They pray; they toss people in peat bogs; they help the sick and injured; they pierce their lips, their noses, ears; they make the same mistakes despite religion, written language, philosophy, and science; they build, they kill, they preserve, they count and figure, they boil the pot, they keep the embers alive; they tell their stories and gird themselves.

Will knowledge you experience directly make you a Buddhist? Must you forfeit excitement per se? To what end?

Say you have seen something. You have seen an ordinary bit of what is real, the infinite fabric of time that eternity shoots through, and time's soft-skinned people working and dying under slowly shifting stars. Then what?

2

Are the Arts and Humanities Your Thing?

How about Science? Do They Halt in the Same Way?

WILSON POON WAS A professor of condensed matter physics at the University of Edinburgh until he was elected to one of the most ancient chairs in the university, that of Natural Philosophy, in 2016. He founded the Edinburgh Complex Fluids Partnership, which works with industry in areas like colloid synthesis, particulate suspensions, and bacteria. In 2019, the Institute of Physics awarded him the Sam Edwards Medal for "the fundamental study of condensed matter physics, statistical physics and biophysics using model colloidal systems." Poon won the 2022 Bingham Medal for rheology.

His coauthor, the late Tom McLeish (1962–2023), was a highly awarded theoretical physicist who ended his distinguished career as the Chair of Natural Philosophy at the University of York.

In this chapter, Poon and McLeish engage with a remarkable book called *Real Presences* by one of the leading literary critics of the twentieth century, George Steiner. Steiner argued that

> any coherent account of the capacity of human speech to com-
> municate meaning and feeling is, in the final analysis, underwrit-
> ten by the assumption of God's existence. I will put forward the
> argument that the experience of aesthetic meaning in particular,

that of literature, of the arts, of musical form, infers the necessary possibility of this "real presence."[1]

Poon and McLeish say the same is so in the sciences.

DISCUSSION QUESTIONS

1. Poon and McLeish write: "The discipline of courtesy inevitably leads one to the discovery of radical otherness."[2] What do they mean by "the discipline of courtesy"? What is "the discovery of radical otherness"? What do these ideas have to do with the humanities and the sciences?

2. Steiner said that in the humanities, "ours is the long day's journey of the Saturday."[3] What did he mean? Why do Poon and McLeish think that science has the same journey?

3. Poon and McLeish write: "Precisely this narrative (and thus 'theoretical'?) shape is refracted by the double lens of cross and resurrection in the New Testament. The obvious resonance with creation and suffering is in the central passage of Romans 8."[4]

    Have a look at Romans 8:18–28 in this lively translation (MSG):

    That's why I don't think there's any comparison between the present hard times and the coming good times. The created world itself can hardly wait for what's coming next. Everything in creation is being more or less held back. God reins it in until both creation and all the creatures are ready and can be released at the same moment into the glorious times ahead. Meanwhile, the joyful anticipation deepens.

    All around us we observe a pregnant creation. The difficult times of pain throughout the world are simply birth pangs. But it's not only around us; it's within us. The Spirit of God is arousing us within. We're also feeling the birth pangs. These sterile and barren bodies of ours are yearning for full deliverance. That is why waiting does not diminish us, any more than waiting diminishes a pregnant mother. We are enlarged in the waiting. We, of course,

---

1. Steiner, *Real Presences*, 3.
2. Poon and McLeish, "Real Presences," this vol., 17.
3. Cited in Poon and McLeish, "Real Presences," this vol., 19.
4. Cited in Poon and McLeish, "Real Presences," this vol., 20.

don't see what is enlarging us. But the longer we wait, the larger we become, and the more joyful our expectancy.

Meanwhile, the moment we get tired in the waiting, God's Spirit is right alongside helping us along. If we don't know how or what to pray, it doesn't matter. He does our praying in and for us, making prayer out of our wordless sighs, our aching groans. He knows us far better than we know ourselves, knows our pregnant condition, and keeps us present before God. That's why we can be so sure that every detail in our lives of love for God is worked into something good.

What connections do you see with what Poon and McLeish, and Steiner, say about the tasks of the humanities and of the sciences?

Real Presences:
Two Scientists' Response to George Steiner

WILSON POON AND TOM MCLEISH

Real Presences is Steiner's personal manifesto against the deconstruction movement in modern literature (and art and music). It is not a book that many scientists would read, let alone reread. And yet we have read and reread the book; it has made us laugh and cry. Why? This essay is a first attempt at articulating the shock of relevance two scientists felt after their encounter with this remarkable book.

I

Real Presences is evidently born out of pain (one reviewer calls it a "vulnerable" book), the pain that Steiner feels deeply in the face of modern deconstructive movements in literature, with their palpable repulse of meaning. Peering over the abyss of linguistic meaninglessness which is our "age of the epilogue" (the "after-Word"), Steiner affirms his belief that the *logos* is meaningful, and that it is meaningful because it is "underwritten" by (at least a wager on) the presence of God.

In contrast to the pain he felt, Steiner asserted recently that "doing first-class science or technology is, visibly, enormous fun . . . it is brimful of laughter and sun-rise."[1] We agree, but in part, because in our experience the "fun" is accompanied by pain; it is brimful of tears and dark shadows as well as "laughter and sun-rise." The shock of relevance we feel upon reading *Real Presences* is twofold: first, that the pain Steiner the literary critic expresses closely parallels the darker side of our experiences as scientists; secondly,

1. Steiner, *Festival Overture*, page number unavailable.

that his suggestions for seeking a way "out of the house of mirrors which is that of modernist theory and practice"[2] have tantalizing resonances with our mental map for a science that hurts less. To find such parallel perceptions is both astonishing and hopeful; astonishing, because the parallels were surely unintended (Steiner repeatedly states that his comments should be *in*applicable to the sciences), and hopeful, because they suggest that meeting at the place of pain may yet prove to be a source of *rapprochement* across the yawning (and painful) chasm between the "Two Cultures"—a practical *theologia crucis* for cultural reconciliation.

II

In part 1 of his book, entitled "A Secondary City," Steiner laments the "Byzantine dominion of secondary and parasitic discourse over immediacy, of the critical over the creative"[3] in today's cultural landscape, whereby we are insulated "from direct encounter with the 'real presence' or the 'real absence of that presence' . . . which an answerable experience of the aesthetic must enforce on us."[4] (For Steiner, "culture" is "literature, art and music"—an irritating pair of blinkers which we are perpetually restrained from removing.) The resonances with felt pain in the present practice of science are immediate: for science today is also dominated by a culture of the secondary. Few progress to the level of the textbook. Those who do find no room for creative maneuver; science consists, for them, of received interpretation and problem-solving. The awe-inspiring contact with primary creation which is the grappling with observation and theory is kept at a safe distance. In parallel to this, there has been an enormous and quite unprecedented explosion of scientific publication in very recent times. Much of this is routine and mediocre, and smells similarly of the secondary.

Steiner described the dominant metaphysic of the age as "journalistic," a metaphysic which confuses "interesting" with "significant." This description finds an urgent echo in the world of politicized science. The five scientific research councils in the UK now routinely talk in terms of "business plans," and subscribe to overtly utilitarian "mission statements" which talk of "enhancing . . . competitiveness and quality of life" (narrowly,

---

2. Steiner, *Real Presences*, 141.

3. Steiner, *Real Presences*, 38.

4. Steiner, *Real Presences*, 39.

that is to say, economically, defined).[5] Much of this smacks of "spurious temporality":[6] "The utmost beauty or terror are shredded at the close of day. We are made whole again, and expectant, in time for the morning edition";[7] or, indeed, the next round of grant applications.

Part 1 contains Steiner's dream of "a society . . . of the primary"[8] dedicated to the creation of primary texts, paintings and compositions and their public or private "performance" (concerts, poetry reading, encountering artwork), however amateur or "professional." We too dream of "a society of the primary," where physical and biological phenomena are once more sources of wonderment and questioning (as they were in the conclusion to Job), where every experience of insight ("Aha, *that's* why the moon shows phases"), however trivial in the eyes of the "professionals," is valued more than the mere recall (the "Master Mind" syndrome) or mechanical manipulation of knowledge. The parallels of analysis and aspiration suggest to us that these two visions, Steiner's and ours, are ultimately one and the same.

III

In part 2, "The Broken Contract," Steiner shows how since the late nineteenth century, the "contract"[9] between *logos* and *kosmos* has lain broken. Before this, "semantic trust"[10] underwrote every utterance. For Steiner, this breaking of the contract is complete with the coming of the modern deconstruction movement, in which words no longer refer to *anything*; instead "what words refer to are [merely] other words," and "the truth of the word is the absence of the world."[11] Here, the painful resonances with the present condition of science are almost spelt out for us by Steiner, when he places deconstruction within an "encompassing background of the crisis of the word"[12] in the modern world, where "larger and larger domains of discovery, of scientific theory, of productive technological appliance have

5. See, for example, EPSRC, "Memorandum."
6. Steiner, *Real Presences*, 26.
7. Steiner, *Real Presences*, 27.
8. Steiner, *Real Presences*, 6.
9. Steiner, *Real Presences*, 93.
10. Steiner, *Real Presences*, 91.
11. Steiner, *Real Presences*, 96–97.
12. Steiner, *Real Presences*, 115.

passed out of reach of verbal articulation and of alphabetic notation";[13] "at the heart of futurity lies [sic] the 'byte' and the number,"[14] not the word. Earlier, in a 1961 essay "The Retreat from the Word," Steiner suggested that the "unspeakability" of modern science was inevitable, quoting the physicist (and atomic bomb builder) J. Robert Oppenheimer as his authority.[15]

That there is wordlessness in the practice of science today is not in doubt. On the one hand, there is manifest mutual incomprehension due to increasing specialization. The rush towards mathematicization by many disciplines, in conscious or unconscious imitation of physics, plunges science across the board into further "unspeakability." On the other hand, there is the infamous inarticulateness of scientists (with notable exceptions). Both manifestations of scientific wordlessness widen the chasm between the "Two Cultures." Wordsworth's prophecy that in the future, science would inspire the sonnets and stanzas of reflection[16] has simply not come true.

We feel such scientific wordlessness confines and diminishes our humanity, and belittles the humanity of those to whom we have fallen silent. We cannot agree with Oppenheimer that any attempt at "speaking" theoretical physics is ultimately an illusion. Meanwhile, the scientific retreat from the word goes some way towards explaining why the public perception of science is fearful, shallow, inaccurate and utilitarian. Much criticism of the decisive role of science[17] is based on a view of the culture which is palpably wrong when seen from the "inside." An inarticulate science lays itself bare to painful misrepresentation: the primary felt activity of questioning is eclipsed by a demand for answers, puzzles by solutions, creativity by control.

Part 2 contains a trenchant discussion of the role of "theory." For Steiner, critical theories are *narratives of formal experience*; they "tell stories of thought."[18] In the age of the "epilogue" (after-Word), however, critical theory, apparently in conscious *"imitatio* of scientific theory," makes "prepotent claims to abstract universality"[19] and to general powers of pre-

13. Steiner, *Real Presences*, 114.

14. Steiner, *Real Presences*, 115.

15. "Retreat from the Word," in Steiner, *Language and Silence*, 12–35.

16. See Carey, *Faber Book of Science*, "Introduction."

17. See, e.g., Appleyard, *Understanding the Present*.

18. Steiner, *Real Presences*, 86; emphasis original.

19. Steiner, *Real Presences*, 74.

diction, and "exalts [itself] above the facts of creation."[20] But what kind of "scientific theory" did Steiner have in mind? It is certainly not the kind with which we are familiar from our own work and from our reading of scientific history. There are indeed narrow areas of physical theory today which make "prepotent claims to abstract universality," and talk of "dreams of a final theory."[21]

Intriguingly these are those areas of science which are most heavily mathematicized. But our mental picture of a main-stream scientific theory is well described in precisely those terms in which Steiner uses to describe the main stream of Western critical theory. The "encircling acts of argument" which we call scientific theories are, fundamentally, narratives (where the insistent reference to words is of the essence); they indeed "recount . . . moments of meeting between intellection and created form, a meeting whose source . . . is always intuitive."[22] For us, a theory is a descriptive explication of that magical moment of "Aha!" All of this has been painfully obscured by the wordlessness at the core of modern science.

IV

The weight of pain felt by Steiner by the end of part 2 of *Real Presences* is almost unbearable. In the midst of the encircling darkness of deconstruction, he seeks a way out. Part 3 of the book, entitled "Presences," starts with a bold positive assertion: "There is language, there is art, because there is 'the other.'"[23] He based this assertion on the observation that "the experiencing of created form is a meeting between freedoms,"[24] between the freedom of creation—"the poem, the sonata, the painting, could very well not be,"[25] and the freedom of reception—"we are utterly free not to receive . . . [when we are] face to face with the presence of offered meaning,"[26] or we are free to make the "gamble of welcome . . . when freedom knocks."[27] Some do make the gamble, and extend the courtesy of welcome to a work

20. Steiner, *Real Presences*, 87.
21. Weinberg, *Dreams of a Final Theory*.
22. Steiner, *Real Presences*, 77.
23. Steiner, *Real Presences*, 137.
24. Steiner, *Real Presences*, 152.
25. Steiner, *Real Presences*, 152.
26. Steiner, *Real Presences*, 152–53.
27. Steiner, *Real Presences*, 156.

of artistic creation. According to Steiner, the "discipline of courtesy"[28] consists of seeking to hear the language of the stranger accurately, "lexical *cortesia*"[29] and being sensitive to "syntax, to the grammars which are the sinew of articulate forms."[30] When we do that, we discover that "we have met before."[31] Moreover, we find that the meeting of freedoms "will always entail approximation . . . A good reading falls short of the text or art object by a distance. The falling-short is a guarantor of the experienced "otherness"—the freedom to be or not to be, to enter into or abstain from a commerce of spirit with us."[32]

Here, Steiner comes so close to making the connection with the process of doing science that watching him not connecting is one of the most painful moments in our reading of *Real Presences*. He comes closest when he compares the "freedom not to be" of the poem, the painting and the sonata with the corresponding "freedom not to be" of the universe. What he says resonates powerfully with our vision of what lies at the core of science:

> The famous question at the roots of metaphysics is: "Why should there not be nothing?"[33] . . .

> Today, mathematical models proclaim access to the origins of the present universe. Molecular biology may have in reach an unravelling of the thread whose beginning is that of life. Nothing in these prodigious conjectures disarms, let alone elucidates, the fact that the world is when it might not have been, the fact that we are in it when we might, when we could not have been.[34]

But what is science? In Steiner's terms it is men and women extending the *cortesia* of welcome to the material universe. But in our experience (and from our reading of scientific biography), the discipline of courtesy inevitably leads one to the discovery of radical otherness, in two senses. First, there is the freedom not to have been: the existence of a universe with as much structure as ours, including forms of organized carbon-based molecules known as life, depends on the very delicate "fine-tuning" of a

28. Steiner, *Real Presences*, 155.

29. Steiner, *Real Presences*, 157.

30. Steiner, *Real Presences*, 158.

31. Steiner, *Real Presences*, 180.

32. Steiner, *Real Presences*, 175.

33. Steiner, *Real Presences*, 152.

34. Steiner, *Real Presences*, 201.

set of physical constants, all of which could, as far as we know, have taken arbitrary values.[35] There is also "otherness" in the encountered sense of strangeness: the progressive loss of anthropocentricity in viewpoint is one of the most persistent themes in scientific history at least since Copernicus removed the earth from the center of the universe.[36] So the pain of disappointment to read "*only art* can go some way towards making accessible, towards waking into some measure of communicability, the sheer inhuman otherness of matter."[37]

Frighteningly, "we are utterly free not to receive . . . [when we are] face to face with the presence of offered meaning which we call a text (or a painting or a symphony)."[38] The same is, of course, true of science. Many exercise their freedom not to receive when face to face with the presence of offered meaning which we call the universe: to witness men and women in our streets simply going about their business as usual (heads decidedly *down*) under the gaze of the magnificent Hale-Bopp comet is heartbreaking.

Steiner's message in part 3 can be summarized thus: "It is the enterprise and privilege of the aesthetic to quicken into lit presence the continuum between temporality and eternity, between matter and spirit, between man and 'the other.'"[39] The echoes with our view of science are loud and clear.

V

Although structured in three parts, *Real Presences* in fact consists of three movements and a coda in a seemingly distant key. In the final two pages, Steiner attempts to set the sweep of his entire thesis within the shape of Judeo-Christian history. The tonal relation between this explicitly theological coda and the rest of Steiner's composition is, to our minds, tantalizingly obscure. Perhaps, even after his own "brilliant cadenzas of argumentation" (John Carey's review in the *Sunday Times*), Steiner still feels overwhelmed by what he sees in the dark abyss of deconstructive meaningless. Earlier he has written, "On its own terms and planes of argument . . . the challenge of deconstruction does seem to me irrefutable."[40] Perhaps he now feels that no

35. Gribbin and Rees, *Cosmic Coincidences.*
36. Weinberg, *Dreams of a Final Theory,* 196.
37. Steiner, *Real Presences,* 175–76.
38. Steiner, *Real Presences,* 153, 156.
39. Steiner, *Real Presences,* 227.
40. Steiner, *Real Presences,* 132.

argument on any plane, however brilliant, can halt the advance of the age of the epilogue (the after-Word). Immediately before the coda in a strange key, we read: "Where it is genuinely immanent . . . the poetics, the art of the 'after-Word' and the interpretative responses they will solicit, will be essentially different from those we have known and whose after-life prevails still, though often either trivialized or made mandarin, in today's transitional circumstances."[41] Night falls on Narnia;[42] and Steiner feels in his bones that the daybreak is going to be long in coming:

> There is one particular day in Western history about which neither historical record nor myth nor Scripture make report. It is a Saturday. And it has become the longest of days. We know of that Good Friday which Christianity holds to have been that of the Cross. But the non-Christian, the atheist, knows of it as well . . . We know, ineluctably, of the pain, of the failure of love, of the solitude which are our history and private fate. We also know about Sunday. To the Christian, that day signifies an intimation . . . of resurrection . . . If we are non-Christians or non-believers, we know of that Sunday in precisely analogous terms . . . the day of liberation from inhumanity and servitude . . . The lineaments of that Sunday carry the name of hope . . .
>
> But ours is the long day's journey of the Saturday. Between suffering, aloneness, unutterable waste on the one hand and the dream of liberation, of rebirth on the other. In the face . . . of the death of love which is Friday, even the greatest art and poetry are almost helpless. In the Utopia of the Sunday, the aesthetic will, presumably, no longer have logic or necessity. The apprehensions and figurations in the play of metaphysical imagining, in the poem and the music, which tell of pain and of hope, of the flesh which is said to taste of ash and the spirit which is said to have the savor of fire, are always Sabbatarian. They have risen out of an immensity of waiting which is that of man. Without them, how could we be patient?[43]

Strangely the distant key of Steiner's coda is precisely that key in which we have been struggling to articulate a "theology of science." To our minds, the "shape" of a Christian understanding of the scientific enterprise does have that same outline of "Friday-Saturday-Sunday." Just as in Steiner's usage, of course, such a narrative shape is just that: an enveloping shorthand

41. Steiner, *Real Presences*, 231.
42. Title of ch. 14 of Lewis, *Last Battle*.
43. Steiner, *Real Presences*, 231–32.

for a richly detailed story. Nonetheless, this shape is set by the most re-markable of ancient Hebrew texts for any reader attuned to the relationship of consciousness seeking understanding of the physical world—the book of Job, and specifically the last three chapters. Here in the context of *suffering*, long promised in the "sweat of the brow" theme of Genesis 3, Job meets with the Creator at last, but unexpectedly: his (and our) questions of injustice are met with a teasing list of mysteries about the physical world. The beauty of the poetry is uncontested but startling for two reasons: this is a poem about science (Wordsworth would have approved), but takes the unusual literary form of *questions*. Questions are pointers; they fuel the narrative of science. Moreover, the encounter is not two-way but three-way: the reason for hope in the otherwise total otherness of creation to human minds is the wel-come of the creator by both. So in the context of the Adamic commission, the teasing questioning of Job 38–40 becomes less of an adumbration and more of an agenda—pointing to a time when people will, in the serpent's words but now appropriately, "be like God, knowing good and evil." In this text, which contains some of the most ancient strands of Hebrew creational thought, we find projected onto the central character the tensions of time between "no longer" and a "not yet." Such a waiting between death and new life is focused much later in the stillness after Easter Friday's bleak afternoon and before the strange freshness of Sunday morning.

Precisely this narrative (and thus "theoretical"?) shape is refracted by the double lens of cross and resurrection in the New Testament. The obvious resonance with creation and suffering is in the central passage of Romans 8. Once more the context of suffering frames the physical creation, which "groans" for liberation from its "bondage to decay." Once more, but now stronger, there is an undercurrent of hope. The final focal point of the shape of human interaction and response to creation is the vision of the Sabbath itself, the new creation of Revelation 21, where (as elsewhere) the dynamic between heaven and earth is *from* heaven *to* earth, not, as fre-quently misunderstood, in the other direction. Now at last is the garden from which mankind was once banished restored and transformed into the new city, and the temporary lights of sun and moon fulfilled in the light of the Creator. Knowledge of the deep structure of the city is complete in all its mineral splendor. After such reconciliation, the creative "groaning" articulated by St. Paul is as (happily) unnecessary as the secondary lights. Essentially, there is no more crying.

So a summary of a biblical theology of our meeting with the material world would say that Science is "a work of the Saturday." Thence springs both its hope and its pain. Thence also the shock of relevance when we follow Steiner on his journey, and to find that at the close of *Real Presences*, he tells us that art, poetry, and music share with science the same admixture of hope and pain, indeed in the same transitional sense: in the fulfilment of their hope they are no longer required. This cannot be coincidence. It points to a way of understanding the relation between the twin cultural responses of humankind which are the arts and the sciences. We have seen, throughout this essay, parallels at the points where the two are suffering. There is the "culture of the secondary" and its dulling intervention between us and the primary in art and science. Steiner tells of a "retreat from the word," a mistrust of implied meaning in language with its consequent abandonment of love ("philology" is a dead discipline). We also feel the pain of the wordlessness in the practice of science today, confining and diminishing our humanity. More hopefully, there is the common "fitful apprehension" of otherness as artists and scientists practice their respective "discipline of courtesy." Finally, there is the astonishing realization that all of this signifies and shares a simple truth which is at once painful and hopeful: "*Ours* [together] *is the long day's journey of the Saturday*."

3

Why Is Philosophy So Impractical?

ROBERTO MANGABEIRA UNGER, A Brazilian, was a precocious student at Harvard Law School. The story goes that in the first week of class, a professor pointed out that a nation's postal service might be organized in many different ways. He suggested to students this was the kind of arcane but conceptually important question that they had never confronted but would at Harvard Law. The twenty-two-year-old Unger raised his hand. He proceeded to give a detailed analysis of postal systems around the world. The shock and awe on the professor's face became the stuff of legend.

Unger is a polymath. He helped found the critical legal studies movement, which shook paradigms in the study of law. He has written iconoclastic works in philosophy, religion, and the foundations of physics. He has served twice in a government role that was virtually created for him: Minister of Strategic Affairs in Brazil, first in 2007 and again in 2015. Roberto Mangabeira Unger puts his ideas on the line.

The optimism and hope underpinning Unger's work run against the grain of postmodern skepticism. Unger claims that every page of his work resounds with "the idea of the infinity of the human spirit, in the individual as well as in humanity."[1] He was raised as a Roman Catholic and, though no longer practicing, remains heavily influenced by Christianity.

"I was brought up as a Christian," he told an interviewer, "and Christianity has ever since remained the grid, the greatest influence on my

1. Unger, *Self Awakened*, 26.

thinking. So, at the center of my ideas is a conception of who we are, a conception very closely related to the Christian view of humanity."[2] His publisher's description of Unger's 2024 book *The World and Us* says, "His central theme is our transcendence, everything in our existence points beyond itself, and its relation to our finitude: everything that surrounds us, and we ourselves, are flawed and ephemeral."

And here is Unger himself, from that book:

> The innermost teaching of Christianity, taken out of the context of its narrative of sacred history, lies in the combination of two themes. The first is the theme of the primacy of love—of love, not altruism—in the organization of our moral experience. The second is the theme of infinity: our participation in God's transcendence and our power to increase, through love, our share in it. In multiple ways, the themes of love and of infinity connect.
>
> We need not believe in the Christian story of creation and redemption to understand and embrace these themes. . . .
>
> What is deepest and most defensible in Christianity is not what offers false escape from the irreparable flaws in the human condition. It is what points to how we can reconcile our transcendence with our finitude, and draw closer to one another, despite those flaws or because of them.[3]

The two readings in this chapter reveal Unger's playful side and his, well, not-so-playful side. The first is the charmer, a letter to graduating sixth graders. The second piece distinguishes classic patterns in metaphysics and in practical philosophy—and what they mean for your life.

DISCUSSION QUESTIONS

1. You might read Unger's letter aloud in a group, and then discuss what in the letter surprises you.

2. In "The Universal Grid of Philosophy," Unger says: "The two overlapping questions that trump all others in the world history of moral thought are: What should I do with my life? and How should I live? . . .

2. Tippett, "Krista Tippett in Conversation," 6:52.
3. Unger, *World and Us*, 250, 254.

There are two main directions the answer to these questions has taken: stay out of trouble and get into trouble; serenity or vulnerability."[4]

Which of those "two main directions" feels closer to the way you now approach life?

3. How do you interpret the final paragraph of "The Universal Grid of Philosophy"?

4. Unger, "Universal Grid of Philosophy," this vol., 35.

A Letter

ROBERTO MANGABEIRA UNGER

Dear —,

When you asked me to write a few words of reflection on your passage from sixth to seventh grade, not for you alone but for all your class, I felt disoriented. We should, whenever possible, speak to what matters and speak from the heart. But how to do so, on an occasion that is neither private nor public, and that invites the discussion of personal truth while repelling the revelation of personal experience? In the end, it seemed best to treat you as the strong and independent spirit you are.

As we pass through childhood, each of us, a storehouse of alternative ways of becoming a person, imagines many different courses of action and of life he may later take. However, we cannot be everything in the world. We must choose a path, and reject other paths. This rejection, indispensable to our self-development, is also a mutilation. In choosing, as we must, we cast aside many aspects of our humanity. If, however, we cast them aside completely, we become less than fully human. We must continue somehow to feel the movements of the limbs we cut off. To learn how to feel them is the first major work of the imagination.

Later on, as adults, we struggle in the world and against it. We settle into a way of living and doing. A mummy begins to form around each of us, diminishing our reach and our vision by accommodating them to our circumstance. We begin to die many small deaths. Our aim should be to die but once. We can continue to live only by breaking out of the mummy. We can break out of it only by denying ourselves some of the safeguards with which we protect ourselves against the frustration of our longings and the defeat of our ambitions.

25

Life comes before goodness, because vitality is the condition of sustained and magnanimous compassion. We are plunged into a great and mysterious darkness, which our minds are able to penetrate only at the edges. Luck and misfortune, beginning with the accident of our birth in a particular class, nation, and community, shape much of what happens to us. We would be almost nothing if we did not fight against the consequences of this fate and recognize in ourselves the unresigned and uncontainable spirits we all really are. By rebelling against our belittlement by the alliance between chance and society, we cease to be little. We become great: unshaken, unsubdued, unterrified.

Our struggle, which is the condition of greatness, would also be the cause of our perversion, were it not transformed by love. To love another person and to be driven by a vision defining a task are the two decisive events a person can experience. They make us godlike. But not just like the God who creates; also like the God who suffers and dies, because through them we also become hostages to other people, who may rebuff our love or destroy our work. This dependence on the others is not our doom. It is our salvation.

All of this is cause for joy. Right now we are both alive. Better you and I not think too much about this fact, or we might be overwhelmed and paralyzed by joy.

Love,

Roberto

The Universal Grid of Philosophy

ROBERTO MANGABEIRA UNGER

In the world history of philosophy, a small number of intellectual options keeps recurring. However, the way in which they recur in the kind of philosophy that proposes to deal with the whole of reality—metaphysics—has been completely different from the way in which they recur in the practical philosophy that deals with social life and human action: politics and ethics.

In metaphysics very little happens, and even less would happen were it not for the influence of two forces. The first force is that philosophers are different, by temperament and circumstance, even before they begin to think and that they are led by ambition as well as by enthusiasm to deepen the differences among themselves. The second force, of increasing significance over the last few centuries, is that natural science changes. Metaphysics must accommodate to such change unless it can force science to temporize, which it almost never can. Because so little happens in metaphysics, metaphysicians can sometimes convince themselves that they have discovered, once and for all, as much of the world as the human mind grasp, by which they generally mean the most important part of the world.

In the practical philosophy of politics and ethics, a few intellectual positions, developed in different vocabularies, have also accounted for the greater part of the most influential ideas. However, much does happen, or can happen, sometimes very quickly. A contest of philosophical positions that may at first seem intractable is in fact resolved in a particular direction, setting thought on a course of cumulative change rather than eternal recurrence or oscillation.

The history of metaphysics has been organized around a single, overriding axis of intellectual alternatives. These alternatives have to do with the relation of being to appearance and therefore also with the relation of being to knowledge. We are more familiar with the expression of the main alternative positions in the categories of our Western philosophical tradition; we first learned from the ancient Greeks the words with which to name them. However, they have close counterparts in Indian and Chinese philosophy as well as in the Arab philosophers who developed the thought of the ancient Greeks in forms different from those that became established in medieval and modern Europe.

At one extreme of this axis lies the idea that the manifest world of distinction and flux is not for real, not at least ultimately. It is an epiphenomenon: an artifact of our perception of the world. Being is one and, insofar as we are real, we form part of it. The theory of the manifest world, in its variety and transformation, is, on this account, an illusion. We can rescue ourselves from this illusion by clinging to what I earlier called by Leibniz's label: the perennial philosophy. Spinoza's *Ethics* presents a version of this view that tries to make sense of the implications of early-modern science.

Further along this axis, in the direction of greater acceptance of the reality of the manifest world is a doctrine of hidden prototypes. Plato's theory of forms (as explored in the *Parmenides*) is the classic instance. There is a hierarchy of forms of being. The distinctions and transformations of the manifest world exhibit a repertory of natural kinds or basic types. All have their origin in the prototypes. The more real the being, the less manifest; the more manifest, the less real. True knowledge, to be won only at great cost, is knowledge of the hidden but plural prototypes rather than of their shadowy and ephemeral expressions in the phenomenal world.

If we move further in the direction of an attempt to save the appearances, to the extreme opposite to the doctrine of being as one, we find that it is not as extreme as we may have expected. The metaphysician as realist, determined to hold firm to the world of the manifest, needs somehow to ground appearance in structure if he is to gain purchase on the reality he seeks to uphold. By so doing, he comes closest to the tenets of the common-sense realism that has always been the trading partner of this metaphysical position: contributing beliefs to it, and receiving them from it.

In the absence of such a structure just beneath the surface of appearance, the mind will dissolve the world of appearance into indistinction; it will lack the means with which to bring the individual phenomena and events under the light of a categorical structure. Consequently, it will begin to lose clarity about the boundaries among them. As they sink into a mush, the effort to save the appearances will risk turning into its supposed opposite, the doctrine of the unity of being. Such an extreme phenomenalism has appeared from time to time in the history of metaphysics, but it has never succeeded in preventing the effort to the appearances from turning against itself.

The solution to this problem in the history of philosophy in many different traditions and civilizations has been to stop one step short of the last step. The metaphysician imagines that just under the surface of appearances there is a structure of kinds. Built into that structure is a set of regularities governing the realization of the kinds in individual phenomena and events. Aristotle's hylomorphism—his doctrine of form and matter—as presented in his *Metaphysics* is the most famous example of such a structure, and the doctrine that each kind tends to the development of the excellence intrinsic to it is the paradigmatic instance of such regularities.

This solution creates, however, another problem. If the structure of kinds and the regime of their realization are not apparent, how are we to prevent them from keeping the ultimate reality of individualized being just beyond our grasp? The individual is the prize—not just the individual person but also the individual phenomenon or event. However, the individual, Aristotle reminded us, is ineffable. Suppose we grasp the particularities of the individual phenomenon or event by subsuming it under a long list of kinds: each kind scoops out a little more of the particularity of the event or the phenomenon. In the end, however, the particularity of the particular remains an unreachable limit. We risk dying of thirst for the real, our idea-laden perceptions outstretched to realities that remain just beyond their reach. From this derivative problem and from the familiar stock of attempted, inconclusive solutions to it there arises a familiar set of disputes in the world history of this metaphysical option.

The natural scientist, or the worshiper of natural science, may attempt to escape this—failure to reach the residue of particularity in the particular—by making two moves. First, he may insist on attributing to the concepts and categories of his science an uncontroversial reality. He may think of them less as conjectures and metaphors, warranted by the interventions and applications they inform, than as part of the furniture of the universe. Second, he may dismiss the individualized remnant of the manifest—the part that fails to be captured by the kinds into which he divides up the world and by the lawlike relations of cause and effect he claims to reveal—as an unimportant residue, a by-product of the marriage of necessity and chance.

It is, however, only by a hallucination that we can mistake the ideas of science for the structure of the world. What dispels this hallucination and returns us to our perplexity is not a metaphysical objection; it is the history of science. Scientific ideas change, sometimes radically. Their periodic subversion saps our ability to convince ourselves that they are nature itself rather than constructions of our minds. Bereft of the consoling hallucination, we find we have sold too cheaply, in exchange for counterfeit goods, the longing to grasp in the mind the particulars of the phenomenal world.

The recurrence of these intellectual alternatives in the history of metaphysics is too universal and too persistent to be marked down to the power of tradition and influence. What Kant said of the antinomies of reason holds true for these conundrums: they result from an overreaching of the mind. The overreaching, however, is not necessary. We can stop it, and so we should.

Meta-physics would better be called meta-humanity. Its secret ambition is that we see ourselves from the outside, from far away and high above, as if we were not ourselves but God. We are, however, not God. We cannot begin to divinize ourselves, little by little, until we acknowledge this fact. The naturalistic prejudice—seeing from the stars—is the beginning of the insuperable problems and of the unsatisfactory options that beset our metaphysical ideas about the relation of being to appearance.

The world history of practical philosophy presents a wholly different situation. Here too we find a small repertory of recurring problems and solutions. Something, however, can happen and has happened that changes everything. Political and ethical thought have no need for meta-humanity. This fact proves to be their salvation.

The central question in political theory is: What does and should hold society together, enabling men and women to enjoy the benefits of social life? There are two limiting solutions. By their extremity and partiality, each turns out to be insufficient. Nevertheless, each contains elements that must be used by any compromise struck in the large middle space these extreme solutions define.

At one limit, the answer to the question is coercion, imposed from above. At the other limit, the answer is love: given by people to one another.

The ruler, having gained power, will put a stop to the relentless struggle of all against all. He will attempt, so far as possible, to achieve a monopoly of violence. He can then offer society its most fundamental good—security, deprived of which people are unable to pursue all other goods.

He who brings the sword soon discovers, however, that he needs additional instruments to rule. For one thing, to consolidate his rule, he must destroy all intermediate organizations just because they are rivals to his power. If, however, society remains unorganized it cannot be easily just because there is no way of delegating a power that in the absence of such delegation may be both omnipresent and ineffectively. For another thing, unless power becomes authority, acquiring legitimacy in the eyes of the ruled, rebellion will lurk always and everywhere. Sooner or later, fear will give way to ambition.

If coercion is not enough, neither is love. People may be bound together by both fellow feeling and erotic attachment. The difficulty lies in assuring both the constancy and the diffusion of this force. It wavers, and, as it moves through a larger social space, it weakens. Fellow feeling weakened becomes trust. Erotic attachment weakened becomes allegiance or loyalty.

Coercion and love are both insufficient. Both, however, are necessary props to the social bond. Both are warm. They must be cooled down. In the cooler, middle space of social life, we find law and contract. Coercive violence is turned into the ultimate, delayed guarantee of institutionalized practice and legal order. Love, diffused and rarified, shades into trust: especially into the ability to trust strangers rather than just other members of a group united by blood.

The rule of law and the experience of trust among strangers, backed ultimately by regulated coercion and diffuse love, are two of the three essential instruments for the preservation of the social bond. Or so we have been taught in the world history of political theory. They are fragile. The different ways of understanding their fragility, and of compensating for it, account for many of the main options in the history of political ideas.

Law becomes more necessary the more different people are from one another and the greater the range of the differences they create. If, however, such differences, of experience, interest, value, and vision, become too great, the shared basis on which the law can be interpreted, elaborated, and applied falls apart. Where law is most needed—in the presence of radical difference of experience and vision—it is least effective.

On the other hand, trust cannot easily dispense with bonds sanctioned—in fact or in imagination—by blood. When it does dispense with them, it is likely to be the low trust required, for example, by the traditional form of the market economy—a simplified form of cooperation among strangers; not the high trust, required as a background to the most advanced practices of cooperation and cooperative experimentalism.

Something must therefore be added to the rule of law and to minimal trust. This third element is the social division of labor, provided by a hierarchy of classes or castes. It is not enough to appeal to brute facts of class society; they must be enveloped in purifying and sanctifying ideas. A widespread conception is that society is naturally divided by classes or ranks, shaped by the distribution of social fates and individual capacities at birth. The belief, common among the ancient Indo-European peoples, of a natural division of society into three major groups—one charged with propitiation and guidance; the second, with fighting and ruling; and the third, with labor and production—is the most important historical example of such a conception.

An account must be provided of why the apparent accident of birth into a certain social rank, with its hereditary prerogatives or disabilities, should be accepted, and why it should be seen to imply a natural distribution of the talents required for the work of each of the social ranks. The position of each person in such a hierarchy of birth may, for example, be determined by what each accomplished or failed to accomplish in a previous life.

The outward hierarchy of classes and castes supports, and in turn draws sustenance from, an inward ordering of the emotions: the right disposition of the different faculties of the human spirit, with reason in command over striving, and striving fueled by bodily appetite and vigor. Social disharmony and moral derangement feed on each other.

The different ways in which law, trust, and the class-bound division of labor can and should be related, against the eternal backgrounds of coercion and love, generate the familiar repertory of problems and positions in the history of political ideas all over the world. It all seems similar, in character although not in content, to the history of metaphysics: a small set of concerns and ideas endlessly recombined in minor variations.

However, it only seems that way until everything changes. What changes everything in the global history of political thought are two connected developments: each of them, at the same time, a shift in our social ideas and a transformation in the practical arrangements of society.

The first development that changes everything is the halting, unfinished destabilization of the idea of class society: of a hierarchical social division of labor, sanctioned by natural necessity if not by sacred authority.

The differences among us, however real, fail to go all the way down. The class organization of society—which, in its weakened, contemporary form, continues to be reproduced by the hereditary transmission of economic and educational advantage through the—is not, according to the new idea, a natural or invariant fact. Its content at any given time and in any given place depends on the nature of the established institutions and the prevailing beliefs.

The vast differences in the measure as well as in the direction of talents among individuals should never override the recognition of our common humanity and the duty of equal respect to which this recognition gives rise. We should not deny or suppress, by failure of material support or moral encouragement, the essential doctrine of a democratic civilization: the constructive genius of ordinary men and women. By improving their cooperative practices and by equipping themselves with more powerful ideas and machines as well as with better practices and institutions, ordinary people can make vast problems yield to the cumulative effects of little solutions. This ingenuity is a homely manifestation of our power to do more than the existing organization of society and culture can readily accommodate.

The second development that changes everything is a sudden, vast enlargement of the assumed repertory of institutional possibilities in the different domains of social life. The implications of the idea that society lacks any natural form assumes their full dimension as we begin to rid ourselves of necessitarian illusions: the illusions of classical European social theory—with its characteristic idea of a predetermined evolutionary sequence of indivisible institutional systems—and of contemporary social science—with its rationalizing trivialization of structural discontinuity in history.

Our interests, ideals, and identities are hostage to the practices and institutions we accept as their practical realization. By motivated and directed tinkering with these arrangements, we force ourselves to revise our understanding of those interests, ideals, and identities. We both illuminate and quicken the dialectic between the reform of society and the revision of our beliefs about ourselves.

The conviction that class division fails to go all the way down joins with the enlargement of the institutional imagination radically to expand our sense of alternatives. One of the consequences of this breakthrough is the ability to develop the four sets of preconditions of the most developed forms of cooperative experimentalism. The result is therefore also to moderate the interference between the two great imperatives of practical progress in social and economic life—cooperation and innovation.

The first condition is the development of the capability-enhancing economic and education endowments. These endowments are shaped by arrangements that, although they withdraw something from the agenda of short-term politics—defined as fundamental rights, only minimally rigidify the surrounding social and economic space. The second condition is subversion of entrenched and extreme inequalities of opportunity as well as rejection of a commitment to rigid equality of resources and circumstances. The third condition is the propagation of an experimentalist impulse through all of society and culture, an impulse nourished by the school. The fourth condition is the preference for discourses and practices that make change endogenous, lessening the dependence of transformation on crisis.

Each of these conditions in turn provides opportunities for experimentation with institutions, practices, and methods. None has a self-evident, uncontroversial institutional expression. Together, they strengthen the practices of experimentalism both directly and indirectly. They do so directly through a loosening of the hold of any closed script on the forms of association. They do so indirectly by making it more likely that in dealing with one another strangers will be able to move beyond the low trust required by the conventional form of the market economy to the high trust demanded by the most fertile cooperative practices.

The marriage of the idea that class division fails to touch the fundamentals of our humanity with the discovery of the institutional indeterminacy of our interests and ideals and indeed of the ideal of society itself puts an end to the endless refrains of political thought. Law and contract as the cooler, feasible middle point between the two impossible warm extremes of coercive order and erotic attachment now become simply the undefined, open space in which to accelerate the reinvention of social life.

A similar shift has taken place for similar reasons in the world history of moral theory. No one could guess from the histories of philosophy written by the professors what the chief line of division in the development of moral thought has in fact been. You might suppose from reading their accounts that it has been some high-order contrast of approach: whether, for example, the overriding concern of moral judgment should be the pursuit of pleasure, the quest for happiness, the achievement of virtue, or the obedience to universal rules. As soon as we begin to examine these supposed contrasts more closely, however, we discover that they begin to collapse into one another.

Then we hit on a more basic weakness of this view of what is at stake in the history of moral philosophy. We can translate any given vision of what to do with a human life into any or all of these seemingly incompatible ethical vocabularies. The message will not be quite the same in each of these translations. Neither, however, will it be clearly different.

The two overlapping questions that trump all others in the world history of moral thought are: What should I do with my life? and How should I live? To the extent that decrees of society and culture have predetermined the choice of life, the second question has been submerged within the first.

There are two main directions the answer to these questions has taken: stay out of trouble and get into trouble; serenity or vulnerability. In the history of moral philosophy, the reasons to take the first direction have until recently seemed overwhelming. Although certain religious teachers began to urge the second direction over two thousand years, their prophecy achieved its present astonishing authority only in the last few hundred years. It has done so by what must be considered the greatest moral revolution in world history.

Faced with the unchanging conditions of human existence, with its rapid march to dissolution in the midst of meaninglessness, the first response is: let us compose ourselves. Let us cast a spell on ourselves that can bring us serenity. Let us detach ourselves from vain striving in a world of shadowy appearances and insubstantial achievements.

It may seem that the doctrine of the epiphenomenal nature of change and distinction and the related idea of the unity of real being—the perennial philosophy—offer the most persuasive metaphysical backdrop for the ethic of serenity. Nevertheless, all the major recurrent positions about the relation of being to appearance—not just the one that denies the reality of change and distinction—have been bent into the service of this ethic of composure. We can see as much by considering the age in which the relation between these metaphysical options and ethical options was most transparent: the Hellenistic period. Before then Aristotle had already combined his apology for contemplative passivity as the experience bringing man closest to the divine with his campaign to vindicate the world of appearances.

We must relate to other people in a way that way that affirms our overriding concern with putting a stop to vain and restless desire. The way to do so has often been to settle into some practice of reciprocal responsibility, recognizing one's duties to other, according to the nature of the relation, as defined by society. A posture of detached and distant benevolence is then most to be desired. This posture may be infused by love. However, it will not be love as the radical acceptance and imagination of the other person and as the demand for such acceptance and imagination, with all its consequent dangers of rejection, misunderstanding, and heartbreak. It will be love as kindness, whenever possible from afar or from on high.

All this changes when there takes place in the moral history of mankind an event that is at once intangible and unique: another vision of human life and its possibilities. The effort to reconcile our need for another with our fear of the jeopardy in which we place one another is now changed by a new insight into the relation between spirit and structure. We recognize ourselves as structure-transcending beings and require more than the middle distance from one another. Our relations are infected—or sublimated—by the unlimited demand for the unlimited.

The goal is no longer composure. It is to live a larger life, for ourselves and for others. To this end, we must change the world—or, at least, part of our immediate world—the better to change ourselves. We must look for trouble. We must be prudent in small things the better to be reckless in big ones. The good we gain from such sacrifices and adventures, and from choosing lead over gold, is priceless: life itself, the ability to continue living and to escape the many small deaths until we die all at once. It is to live more fully as the infinite imprisoned within the finite that we really are. It is to begin the work of our divinization without denying the inalterable circumstances of our existence.

On the way, as the moral thinking of humanity begins to move in this direction, and to abandon the ideal of a serenity at once deathless and lifeless, there comes the moment of universalizing obligation, of Kant's categorical imperative. It is a movement toward the other person, but under the distancing shield of moral law, with the hypochondriac's fear of others and the ascetic's fear of the body and its desires, as if incarnate spirit would read from a rule book and wear an undershirt.

The acceptance of personal vulnerability and the struggle for world transformation (however small the part of the world thus changed) for the sake of self-transformation, and for self-transformation for the sake of world transformation, become organizing ideals of life. This way of thinking had two roots. Over time these two roots become entangled in each other. One root lies in the history of our moral ideas, interrupted and redirected by prophetic inspiration and religious revolution. The other root lies in the progress of democracy and in the consequent loosening of the hold of any entrenched scheme of social division and hierarchy over what we expect and demand from one another.

A breakthrough bearing a message of universal value to humanity, such as the message conveyed by this world-historical reorientation in political and moral thought, cannot be the privileged possession of any civilization or any time. If indeed we can never be completely imprisoned by a society or a culture, such a message will have been anticipated in the countercurrents of even those times and situations that seem most alien or antagonistic to it. Long after the contests produced by the spread of the message, scholars will look back and say, for example: see, the thinkers of pre-imperial China shared similar concerns and made similar proposals. And indeed if the truth revealed by the turn is deep and strong people must have recognized it—often only dimly but sometimes more clearly—always and everywhere.

Yet if time, change, and difference are for real and if history is as dangerous and decisive as it seems to be, the discovery and propagation of this universal message must have become entangled in the scandalous particularity of historical experience: carried by particular agents, in particular situations, through experiences of conflict and conversion that turned a precarious countercurrent into a triumphant creed. The particularity missing from the message belongs in spades to the plot. We have to take care only that the particulars of the plot—its passage through particular nations, cultures, classes, and individuals—not contaminate the universality of the message. The plot, full of surprise, accident, and paradoxical reversals, reminds us that embodied spirit must bear all the weight of a world of particulars—including the weight of imperial power and of resistance to it. Who would hear truth from the conqueror or accept wisdom from those who refuse to give recognition? It is, however, a fact intimately related to the insights conveyed by this change in the direction of political and moral thought that our traditions and civilizations are not for keeps. Although they help make us who we are, we, in the end, are not they, if only because they are finite and we are not. In the worldwide competition and emulation of the present time, the distinct national cultures are in the process of being jumbled up and emptied out. In the contest of cultures the waning of actual difference arouses all the more the enraged will to difference. Emptied of content national cultures cannot be objects of half-deliberate compromise, as they had been when they lived as detailed customary ways of life. There is less and less to compromise; only an assertion of willed difference, made the more poisonous by having been deprived of tangible content.

The solution, however, is not to preserve these traditions and civilizations as fossils under a glass. It is to replace the fictions of the collective will to difference by institutions and practices that strengthen the collective ability to produce real differences: distinct forms of life, realized through different institutional orders. It is to reinterpret the role of nations in a world of democracies as a form of moral specialization within humanity: the development of our powers in different directions and the realization of a democratic society in alternative sets of arrangements. It is to obey the law of the spirit, according to which we can possess only what we reinvent, and reinvent only what we renounce. The combination of the moral and the political turns breaks the world-historical mold of philosophy. The two turns, combined, abandon metaphysics to its routines, barely modified by the tenets of present-day science. But they change our ideas about ourselves forever.

What is the conclusion to draw from this inquiry into the universal grid of philosophy? It is that we cannot become God and that we can become more godlike.

4

We Human Beings Are Vanishingly
Small and Impermanent

Life Is Meaningless. Isn't it?

WILLIAM JAMES (1842–1910) HAS been called America's first psychologist and first philosopher. As a young man, he was an artist. In medical school, he explored the Amazon with the great biologist Louis Agassiz. James was interested and engaged in everything from laboratory science to the Anti-Imperialist League to parapsychology. And he had a sense of humor.

This chapter comes from James's *The Will to Believe*. In the title essay in that book, James distinguishes the statements of science, ethics, and religion:

> Science says things are; morality says some things are better than other things; and religion says essentially two things.
>
> First, she says that the best things are the more eternal things, the overlapping things, the things in the universe that throw the last stone, so to speak, and say the final word. "Perfection is eternal,"—this phrase of Charles Secrétan seems a good way of putting this first affirmation of religion, an affirmation which obviously cannot yet be verified scientifically at all.
>
> The second affirmation of religion is that we are better off even now if we believe her first affirmation to be true.[1]

---

1. James, *Will to Believe*, 25–26.

James's magisterial *Varieties of Religious Experience* (1902) is full of trenchant, amusing stories and analyses. In his descriptions, you may recognize friends and relatives—and possibly yourself. With all his use of anecdotes, overall James takes a scientific, empirical approach to religious experience—as opposed, say, to a theoretical or dogmatic one. One of his findings: "This readiness for great things, and this sense that the world by its importance, wonderfulness, etc., is apt for their production, would seem to be the undifferentiated germ of all the higher faiths."[2]

The present chapter was originally an address to the Harvard Young Men's Christian Association. His audience was mostly young intellectuals.

> Many of you . . . have already felt in your own persons the skepticism and unreality that too much grubbing in the abstract roots of things will breed. This is, indeed, one of the regular fruits of the over-studious career. Too much questioning and too little active responsibility lead, almost as often as too much sensualism does, to the edge of the slope, at the bottom of which lie pessimism and the nightmare or suicidal view of life. But to the diseases which reflection breeds, still further reflection can oppose effective remedies.[3]

DISCUSSION QUESTIONS

1. In your experience, do many people address the big questions of life simply through a kind of congenital optimism or pessimism? What about you?

2. Discuss: "But those times are past, and we of the nineteenth century, with our evolutionary theories and our mechanical philosophies, already know nature too impartially and too well to worship unreservedly any god of whose character she can be an adequate expression."[4]

3. Consider this passage: "If this life be not a real fight, in which something is eternally gained for the Universe by success, it is no better than a game of private theatricals from which one may withdraw at will. But it *feels* like a real fight; as if there were something really wild

2. James, *Varieties of Religious Experience*, 506n.
3. James, "Is Life Worth Living," this vol., 47.
4. James, "Is Life Worth Living," this vol., 50.

in the Universe which we, with all our idealities and faithfulnesses, are needed to redeem."[5]

In your life, where do you see "a game of private theatricals"? Where "a real fight" that you feel you are "needed to redeem"?

---

5. James, "Is Life Worth Living," this vol., 61; emphasis original.

Is Life Worth Living?

WILLIAM JAMES

When Mr. Mallock's book with this title appeared some fifteen years ago, the jocose answer that "it depends on the *liver*" had great currency in the newspapers. The answer which I propose to give to-night cannot be jocose. In the words of one of Shakespeare's prologues, "I come no more to make you laugh; things now, that bear a weighty and a serious brow, sad, high, and working, full of state and woe," must be my theme. In the deepest heart of all of us there is a corner in which the ultimate mystery of things works sadly; and I know not what such an association as yours intends, nor what you ask of those whom you invite to address you, unless it be to lead you from the surface glamour of existence, and for an hour at least to make you heedless to the buzzing and jigging and vibration of small interests and excitements that form the tissue of our ordinary consciousness. Without further explanation or apology, then, I ask you to join me in turning an attention, commonly too unwilling, to the profounder bass note of life. Let us search the lonely depths for an hour together, and see what answers in the last folds and recesses of things our question may find.

I

With many men the question of life's worth is answered by a temperamental optimism which makes them incapable of believing that anything seriously evil can exist. Our dear old Walt Whitman's works are the standing textbook of this kind of optimism. The mere joy of living is so immense in Walt Whitman's veins that it abolishes the possibility of any other kind of feeling:—

To breathe the air, how delicious!
To speak, to walk, to seize something by the hand! . . .
To be this incredible God I am! . . .
O amazement of things, even the least particle!
O spirituality of things!
I too carol the Sun, usher'd or at noon, or as now, setting;
I too throb to the brain and beauty of the earth and of all the
growths of the earth . . .
I sing to the last the equalities, modern or old,
I sing the endless finales of things,
I say Nature continues—glory continues.
I praise with electric voice,
For I do not see one imperfection in the universe,
And I do not see one cause or result lamentable at last.

So Rousseau, writing of the nine years he spent at Annecy, with nothing but his happiness to tell:

How tell what was neither said nor done nor even thought, but
tasted only and felt, with no object of my felicity but the emotion
of felicity itself! I rose with the sun, and I was happy; I went to
walk, and I was happy; I saw "Maman," and I was happy; I left her,
and I was happy. I rambled through the woods and over the vine-
slopes, I wandered in the valleys, I read, I lounged, I worked in the
garden, I gathered the fruits, I helped at the indoor work, and happiness followed me everywhere. It was in no one assignable thing;
it was all within myself; it could not leave me for a single instant.

If moods like this could be made permanent, and constitutions like
these universal, there would never be any occasion for such discourses as
the present one. No philosopher would seek to prove articulately that life
is worth living, for the fact that it absolutely is so would vouch for itself,
and the problem disappear in the vanishing of the question rather than
in the coming of anything like a reply. But we are not magicians to make
the optimistic temperament universal; and alongside of the deliverances
of temperamental optimism concerning life, those of temperamental pessimism always exist, and oppose to them a standing refutation. In what is
called "circular insanity," phases of melancholy succeed phases of mania,
with no outward cause that we can discover; and often enough to one and
the same well person life will present incarnate radiance today and incarnate dreariness tomorrow, according to the fluctuations of what the older
medical books used to call "the concoction of the humors." In the words

of the newspaper joke, "it depends on the liver." Rousseau's ill-balanced constitution undergoes a change, and behold him in his latter evil days a prey to melancholy and black delusions of suspicion and fear. Some men seem launched upon the world even from their birth with souls as incapable of happiness as Walt Whitman's was of gloom, and they have left us their messages in even more lasting verse than his—the exquisite Leopardi, for example; or our own contemporary, James Thomson, in that pathetic book, *The City of Dreadful Night*, which I think is less well known than it should be for its literary beauty, simply because men are afraid to quote its words—they are so gloomy, and at the same time so sincere. In one place the poet describes a congregation gathered to listen to a preacher in a great unillumined cathedral at night. The sermon is too long to quote, but it ends thus:—

> "O Brothers of sad lives! they are so brief;
> A few short years must bring us all relief:
> Can we not bear these years of laboring breath.
> But if you would not this poor life fulfil,
> Lo, you are free to end it when you will,
> Without the fear of waking after death."—
> The organ-like vibrations of his voice
> Thrilled through the vaulted aisles and died away;
> The yearning of the tones which bade rejoice
> Was sad and tender as a requiem lay:
> Our shadowy congregation rested still,
> As brooding on that "End it when you will."
> * * * * *
> Our shadowy congregation rested still,
> As musing on that message we had heard,
> And brooding on that "End it when you will,"
> Perchance awaiting yet some other word;
> When keen as lightning through a muffled sky
> Sprang forth a shrill and lamentable cry;—
> "The man speaks sooth, alas! the man speaks sooth:
> We have no personal life beyond the grave;
> There is no God; Fate knows nor wrath nor ruth:
> Can I find here the comfort which I crave?
> "In all eternity I had one chance,
> One few years' term of gracious human life—
> The splendors of the intellect's advance,
> The sweetness of the home with babes and wife;
> "The social pleasures with their genial wit;

44

The fascination of the worlds of art;
The glories of the worlds of Nature lit
By large imagination's glowing heart;
"The rapture of mere being, full of health;
The careless childhood and the ardent youth;
The strenuous manhood winning various wealth,
The reverend age serene with life's long truth;
"All the sublime prerogatives of Man;
The storied memories of the times of old,
The patient tracking of the world's great plan
Through sequences and changes myriadfold.
"This chance was never offered me before;
For me the infinite past is blank and dumb;
This chance recurreth never, nevermore;
Blank, blank for me the infinite To-come.
"And this sole chance was frustrate from my birth,
A mockery, a delusion; and my breath
Of noble human life upon this earth
So racks me that I sigh for senseless death.
"My wine of life is poison mixed with gall,
My noonday passes in a nightmare dream,
I worse than lose the years which are my all:
What can console me for the loss supreme?
"Speak not of comfort where no comfort is,
Speak not at all: can words make foul things fair!
Our life's a cheat, our death a black abyss:
Hush, and be mute, envisaging despair."
This vehement voice came from the northern aisle,
Rapid and shrill to its abrupt harsh close;
And none gave answer for a certain while,
For words must shrink from these most wordless woes;
At last the pulpit speaker simply said,
With humid eyes and thoughtful, drooping head—
"My Brother, my poor Brothers, it is thus:
This life holds nothing good for us,
But it ends soon and nevermore can be;
And we knew nothing of it ere our birth,
And shall know nothing when consigned to earth;
I ponder these thoughts, and they comfort me."

"It ends soon, and never more can be," "Lo, you are free to end it when you will,"—these verses flow truthfully from the melancholy Thomson's pen, and are in truth a consolation for all to whom, as to him, the world is far more like a steady den of fear than a continual fountain of delight. That life is not worth living the whole army of suicides declare—an army whose roll-call, like the famous evening gun of the British army, follows the sun round the world and never terminates. We, too, as we sit here in our comfort, must "ponder these things" also, for we are of one substance with these suicides, and their life is the life we share. The plainest intellectual integrity—nay, more, the simplest manliness and honor, forbid us to forget their case.

"If suddenly," says Mr. Ruskin, "in the midst of the enjoyments of the palate and lightnesses of heart of a London dinner-party, the walls of the chamber were parted, and through their gap the nearest human beings who were famishing and in misery were borne into the midst of the company feasting and fancy free; if, pale from death, horrible in destitution, broken by despair, body by body they were laid upon the soft carpet, one beside the chair of every guest—would only the crumbs of the dainties be cast to them; would only a passing glance, a passing thought, be vouchsafed to them? Yet the actual facts, the real relation of each Dives and Lazarus, are not altered by the intervention of the house-wall between the table and the sick-bed—by the few feet of ground (how few!) which are, indeed, all that separate the merriment from the misery."

II

To come immediately to the heart of my theme, then, what I propose is to imagine ourselves reasoning with a fellow-mortal who is on such terms with life that the only comfort left him is to brood on the assurance, "You may end it when you will." What reasons can we plead that may render such a brother (or sister) willing to take up the burden again? Ordinary Christians, reasoning with would-be suicides, have little to offer them beyond the usual negative, "Thou shalt not." God alone is master of life and death, they say, and it is a blasphemous act to anticipate his absolving hand. But can *we* find nothing richer or more positive than this, no reflections to urge whereby the suicide may actually see, and in all sad seriousness feel, that in spite of adverse appearances even for him life is still worth living? There are suicides and suicides (in the United States about three thousand of them every year), and I must frankly confess that with perhaps the majority of these my suggestions are impotent to deal. Where suicide is the result of insanity or sudden frenzied impulse, reflection is impotent to arrest its headway; and cases like these belong to the ultimate mystery of evil, concerning which I can only offer considerations tending toward religious patience at the end of this hour. My task, let me say now, is practically narrow, and my words are to deal only with that metaphysical *tedium vitae* which is peculiar to reflecting men. Most of you are devoted, for good or ill, to the reflective life. Many of you are students of philosophy, and have already felt in your own persons the skepticism and unreality that too much grubbing in the abstract roots of things will breed. This is, indeed, one of the regular fruits of the over-studious career. Too much questioning and too little active responsibility lead, almost as often as too much sensualism does, to the edge of the slope, at the bottom of which lie pessimism and the nightmare or suicidal view of life. But to the diseases which reflection breeds, still further reflection can oppose effective remedies; and it is of the melancholy and *Weltschmerz* bred of reflection that I now proceed to speak.

Let me say, immediately, that my final appeal is to nothing more recondite than religious faith. So far as my argument is to be destructive, it will consist in nothing more than the sweeping away of certain views that often keep the springs of religious faith compressed; and so far as it is to be constructive, it will consist in holding up to the light of day certain considerations calculated to let loose these springs in a normal, natural way. Pessimism is essentially a religious disease. In the form of it to which you are most liable, it consists in nothing but a religious demand to which there comes no normal religious reply.

Now, there are two stages of recovery from this disease, two different levels upon which one may emerge from the midnight view to the daylight view of things, and I must treat of them in turn. The second stage is the more complete and joyous, and it corresponds to the freer exercise of religious trust and fancy. There are, as is well known, persons who are naturally very free in this regard, others who are not at all so. There are persons, for instance, whom we find indulging to their heart's content in prospects of immortality; and there are others who experience the greatest difficulty in making such a notion seem real to themselves at all. These latter persons are tied to their senses, restricted to their natural experience; and many of them, moreover, feel a sort of intellectual loyalty to what they call "hard facts," which is positively shocked by the easy excursions into the unseen that other people make at the bare call of sentiment. Minds of either class may, however, be intensely religious. They may equally desire atonement and reconciliation, and crave acquiescence and communion with the total soul of things. But the craving, when the mind is pent in to the hard facts, especially as science now reveals them, can breed pessimism, quite as easily as it breeds optimism when it inspires religious trust and fancy to wing their way to another and a better world.

That is why I call pessimism an essentially religious disease. The nightmare view of life has plenty of organic sources; but its great reflective source has at all times been the contradiction between the phenomena of nature and the craving of the heart to believe that behind nature there is a spirit whose expression nature is. What philosophers call "natural theology" has been one way of appeasing this craving; that poetry of nature in which our English literature is so rich has been another way. Now, suppose a mind of the latter of our two classes, whose imagination is pent in consequently, and who takes its facts "hard;" suppose it, moreover, to feel strongly the craving for communion, and yet to realize how desperately difficult it is to construe the scientific order of nature either theologically or poetically—and what result can there be but inner discord and contradiction? Now, this inner discord (merely as discord) can be relieved in either of two ways: The longing to read the facts religiously may cease, and leave the bare facts by themselves; or, supplementary facts may be discovered or believed-in, which permit the religious reading to go on. These two ways of relief are the two stages of recovery, the two levels of escape from pessimism, to which I made allusion a moment ago, and which the sequel will, I trust, make more clear.

III

Starting then with nature, we naturally tend, if we have the religious craving, to say with Marcus Aurelius, "O Universe! what thou wishest I wish." Our sacred books and traditions tell us of one God who made heaven and earth, and, looking on them, saw that they were good. Yet, on more intimate acquaintance, the visible surfaces of heaven and earth refuse to be brought by us into any intelligible unity at all. Every phenomenon that we would praise there exists cheek by jowl with some contrary phenomenon that cancels all its religious effect upon the mind. Beauty and hideousness, love and cruelty, life and death keep house together in indissoluble partnership; and there gradually steals over us, instead of the old warm notion of a man-loving Deity, that of an awful power that neither hates nor loves, but rolls all things together meaninglessly to a common doom. This is an uncanny, a sinister, a nightmare view of life, and its peculiar *Unheimlichkeit*, or poisonousness, lies expressly in our holding two things together which cannot possibly agree—in our clinging, on the one hand, to the demand that there shall be a living spirit of the whole; and, on the other, to the belief that the course of nature must be such a spirit's adequate manifestation and expression. It is in the contradiction between the supposed being of a spirit that encompasses and owns us, and with which we ought to have some communion, and the character of such a spirit as revealed by the visible world's course, that this particular death-in-life paradox and this melancholy-breeding puzzle reside, Carlyle expresses the result in that chapter of his immortal *Sartor Resartus* entitled "The Everlasting No." "I lived," writes poor Teufelsdroeckh, "in a continual, indefinite, pining fear; tremulous, pusillanimous, apprehensive of I knew not what: it seemed as if all things in the heavens above and the earth beneath would hurt me; as if the heavens and the earth were but boundless jaws of a devouring monster, wherein I, palpitating, lay waiting to be devoured."

This is the first stage of speculative melancholy. No brute can have this sort of melancholy; no man who is irreligious can become its prey. It is the sick shudder of the frustrated religious demand, and not the mere necessary outcome of animal experience. Teufelsdroeckh himself could have made shift to face the general chaos and bedevilment of this world's experiences very well, were he not the victim of an originally unlimited trust and affection towards them. If he might meet them piecemeal, with no suspicion of any whole expressing itself in them, shunning the bitter parts and husbanding the sweet ones, as the occasion served, and as the day was foul or fair, he could have zigzagged toward an easy end, and felt no obligation to make the air vocal with his lamentations. The mood of levity, of "I don't care," is for this world's ills a sovereign and practical anesthetic. But, no! something deep down in Teufelsdroeckh and in the rest of us tells us that there *is* a Spirit in things to which we owe allegiance, and for whose sake we must keep up the serious mood. And so the inner fever and discord also are kept up; for nature taken on her visible surface reveals no such Spirit, and beyond the facts of nature we are at the present stage of our inquiry not supposing ourselves to look.

Now, I do not hesitate frankly and sincerely to confess to you that this real and genuine discord seems to me to carry with it the inevitable bankruptcy of natural religion naively and simply taken. There were times when Leibnitzes with their heads buried in monstrous wigs could compose Theodicies, and when stall-fed officials of an established church could prove by the valves in the heart and the round ligament of the hip-joint the existence of a "Moral and Intelligent Contriver of the World." But those times are past; and we of the nineteenth century, with our evolutionary theories and our mechanical philosophies, already know nature too impartially and too well to worship unreservedly any God of whose character she can be an adequate expression. Truly, all we know of good and duty proceeds from nature; but none the less so all we know of evil. Visible nature is all plasticity and indifference—a moral multiverse, as one might call it, and not a moral universe. To such a harlot we owe no allegiance; with her as a whole we can establish no moral communion; and we are free in our dealings with her several parts to obey or destroy, and to follow no law but that of prudence in coming to terms with such other particular features as will help us to our private ends. If there be a divine Spirit of the universe, nature, such as we know her, cannot possibly be its *ultimate word* to man. Either there is no Spirit revealed in nature, or else it is inadequately revealed there; and (as all the higher religions have assumed) what we call visible nature, or *this* world, must be but a veil and surface-show whose full meaning resides in a supplementary unseen or *other* world.

I cannot help, therefore, accounting it on the whole a gain (though it may seem for certain poetic constitutions a very sad loss) that the naturalistic superstition, the worship of the God of nature, simply taken as such, should have begun to loosen its hold upon the educated mind. In fact, if I am to express my personal opinion unreservedly, I should say (in spite of its sounding blasphemous at first to certain ears) that the initial step towards getting into healthy ultimate relations with the universe is the act of rebellion against the idea that such a God exists. Such rebellion essentially is that which in the chapter I have quoted from Carlyle goes on to describe:—

> "Wherefore, like a coward, dost thou forever pip and whimper, and go cowering and trembling? Despicable biped! . . . Hast thou not a heart; canst thou not suffer whatsoever it be; and, as a Child of Freedom, though outcast, trample Tophet itself under thy feet, while it consumes thee? Let it come, then, I will meet it and defy it!" And as I so thought, there rushed like a stream of fire over my whole soul; and I shook base Fear away from me forever . . .
> Thus had the Everlasting No pealed authoritatively through all the recesses of my being, of my Me, and then was it that my whole Me stood up, in native God-created majesty, and recorded its Protest. Such a Protest, the most important transaction in life, may that same Indignation and Defiance, in a psychological point of view,

be fitly called. The Everlasting No had said: "Behold, thou art fatherless, outcast, and the Universe is mine"; to which my whole Me now made answer: "I am not thine, but Free, and forever hate thee!"

From that hour, Teufelsdroeckh-Carlyle adds, "I began to be a man." And our poor friend, James Thomson, similarly writes:—

> Who is most wretched in this dolorous place?
> I think myself, yet I would rather be
> My miserable self than He, than He
> Who formed such creatures to his own disgrace.
> The vilest thing must be less vile than Thou
> From whom it had its being, God and Lord!
> Creator of all woe and sin! abhorred,
> Malignant and implacable! I vow
> That not for all Thy power furled and unfurled,
> For all the temples to Thy glory built,
> Would I assume the ignominious guilt
> Of having made such men in such a world.

We are familiar enough in this community with the spectacle of persons exulting in their emancipation from belief in the God of their ancestral Calvinism—him who made the garden and the serpent, and pre-appointed the eternal fires of hell. Some of them have found humaner gods to worship, others are simply converts from all theology; but, both alike, they assure us that to have got rid of the sophistication of thinking they could feel any reverence or duty toward that impossible idol gave a tremendous happiness to their souls. Now, to make an idol of the spirit of nature, and worship it, also leads to sophistication; and in souls that are religious and would also be scientific the sophistication breeds a philosophical melancholy, from which the first natural step of escape is the denial of the idol; and with the downfall of the idol, whatever lack of positive joyousness may remain, there comes also the downfall of the whimpering and cowering mood. With evil simply taken as such, men can make short work, for their relations with it then are only practical. It looms up no longer so spectrally, it loses all its haunting and perplexing significance, as soon as the mind attacks the instances of it singly, and ceases to worry about their derivation from the "one and only Power."

Here, then, on this stage of mere emancipation from monistic superstition, the would-be suicide may already get encouraging answers to his question about the worth of life. There are in most men instinctive springs of vitality that respond healthily when the burden of metaphysical and infinite responsibility rolls off. The certainty that you now *may* step out of life whenever you please, and that to do so is not blasphemous or monstrous, is itself an immense relief. The thought of suicide is now no longer a guilty challenge and obsession.

> "This little life is all we must endure;
> The grave's most holy peace is ever sure,"—

says Thomson; adding, "I ponder these thoughts, and they comfort me." Meanwhile we can always stand it for twenty-four hours longer, if only to see what tomorrow's newspaper will contain, or what the next postman will bring.

But far deeper forces than this mere vital curiosity are arousable, even in the pessimistically-tending mind; for where the loving and admiring impulses are dead, the hating and fighting impulses will still respond to fit appeals. This evil which we feel so deeply is something that we can also help to overthrow; for its sources, now that no "Substance" or "Spirit" is behind them, are finite, and we can deal with each of them in turn. It is, indeed, a remarkable fact that sufferings and hardships do not, as a rule, abate the love of life; they seem, on the contrary, usually to give it a keener zest. The sovereign source of melancholy is repletion. Need and struggle are what excite and inspire us; our hour of triumph is what brings the void. Not the Jews of the captivity, but those of the days of Solomon's glory are those from whom the pessimistic utterances in our Bible come. Germany, when she lay trampled beneath the hoofs of Bonaparte's troopers, produced perhaps the most optimistic and idealistic literature that the world has seen; and not till the French "milliards" were distributed after 1871 did pessimism overrun the country in the shape in which we see it there today. The history of our own race is one long commentary on the cheerfulness that comes with fighting ills. Or take the Waldenses, of whom I lately have been reading, as examples of what strong men will endure. In 1483 a papal bull of Innocent VIII enjoined their extermination. It absolved those who should take up the crusade against them from all ecclesiastical pains and penalties, released them from any oath, legitimized their title to all property which they might have illegally acquired, and promised remission of sins to all who should kill the heretics.

"There is no town in Piedmont," says a Vaudois writer, "where some of our brethren have not been put to death. Jordan Terbano was burnt alive at Susa; Hippolite Rossiero at Turin, Michael Goneto, an octogenarian, at Sarcena; Vilermin Ambrosio hanged on the Col di Meano; Hugo Chiambs, of Fenestrelle, had his entrails torn from his living body at Turin; Peter Geymarali of Bobbio in like manner had his entrails taken out in Lucerna, and a fierce cat thrust in their place to torture him further; Maria Romano was buried alive at Rocca Patia; Magdalena Fauno underwent the same fate at San Giovanni; Susanna Michelini was bound hand and foot, and left to perish of cold and hunger on the snow at Sarcena; Bartolomeo Fache, gashed with sabres, had the wounds filled up with quicklime, and perished thus in agony at Penile; Daniel Michelini had his tongue torn out at Bobbo for having praised God; James Baridari perished covered with sulphurous matches which had been forced into his flesh under the nails, between the fingers, in the nostrils, in the lips, and all over the body, and then lighted; Daniel Rovelli had his mouth filled with gunpowder, which, being lighted, blew his head to pieces; . . . Sara Rostignol was slit open from the legs to the bosom, and left so to perish on the road between Eyral and Lucerna; Anna Charbonnier was impaled, and carried thus on a pike from San Giovanni to La Torre."[1]

Und dergleichen mehr! In 1630 the plague swept away one half of the Vaudois population, including fifteen of their seventeen pastors. The places of these were supplied from Geneva and Dauphiny, and the whole Vaudois people learned French in order to follow their services. More than once their number fell, by unremitting persecution, from the normal standard of twenty-five thousand to about four thousand. In 1686 the Duke of Savoy ordered the three thousand that remained to give up their faith or leave the country. Refusing, they fought the French and Piedmontese armies till only eighty of their fighting men remained alive or uncaptured, when they gave up, and were sent in a body to Switzerland. But in 1689, encouraged by William of Orange and led by one of their pastor-captains, between eight hundred and nine hundred of them returned to conquer their old homes again. They fought their way to Bobi, reduced to four hundred men in the first half year, and met every force sent against them, until at last the Duke of Savoy, giving up his alliance with that abomination of desolation, Louis XIV, restored them to comparative freedom—since which time they have increased and multiplied in their barren Alpine valleys to this day.

1. Quoted by George E. Waring in his book on Tyrol, *Tyrol and the Skirt.* Compare Bérard, *Vaudois.*

What are our woes and sufferance compared with these? Does not the recital of such a fight so obstinately waged against such odds fill us with resolution against our petty powers of darkness—machine politicians, spoilsmen, and the rest? Life is worth living, no matter what it bring, if only such combats may be carried to successful terminations and one's heel set on the tyrant's throat. To the suicide, then, in his supposed world of multifarious and immoral nature, you can appeal—and appeal in the name of the very evils that make his heart sick there—to wait and see his part of the battle out. And the consent to live on, which you ask of him under these circumstances, is not the sophistical "resignation" which devotees of cowering religions preach: it is not resignation in the sense of licking a despotic Deity's hand. It is, on the contrary, a resignation based on manliness and pride. So long as your would-be suicide leaves an evil of his own unremedied, so long he has strictly no concern with evil in the abstract and at large. The submission which you demand of yourself to the general fact of evil in the world, your apparent acquiescence in it, is here nothing but the conviction that evil at large is *none of your business* until your business with your private particular evils is liquidated and settled up. A challenge of this sort, with proper designation of detail, is one that need only be made to be accepted by men whose normal instincts are not decayed; and your reflective would-be suicide may easily be moved by it to face life with a certain interest again. The sentiment of honor is a very penetrating thing. When you and I, for instance, realize how many innocent beasts have had to suffer in cattle-cars and slaughter-pens and lay down their lives that we might grow up, all fattened and clad, to sit together here in comfort and carry on this discourse, it does, indeed, put our relation to the universe in a more solemn light. "Does not," as a young Amherst philosopher (Xenos Clark, now dead) once wrote, "the acceptance of a happy life upon such terms involve a point of honor?" Are we not bound to take some suffering upon ourselves, to do some self-denying service with our lives, in return for all those lives upon which ours are built? To hear this question is to answer it in but one possible way, if one have a normally constituted heart.

Thus, then, we see that mere instinctive curiosity, pugnacity, and honor may make life on a purely naturalistic basis seem worth living from day to day to men who have cast away all metaphysics in order to get rid of hypochondria, but who are resolved to owe nothing as yet to religion and its more positive gifts. A poor halfway stage, some of you may be inclined to say; but at least you must grant it to be an honest stage; and no man should dare to speak meanly of these instincts which are our nature's best equipment, and to which religion herself must in the last resort address her own peculiar appeals.

IV

And now, in turning to what religion may have to say to the question, I come to what is the soul of my discourse. Religion has meant many things in human history; but when from now onward I use the word I mean to use it in the supernaturalist sense, as declaring that the so-called order of nature, which constitutes this world's experience, is only one portion of the total universe, and that there stretches beyond this visible world an unseen world of which we now know nothing positive, but in its relation to which the true significance of our present mundane life consists. A man's religious faith (whatever more special items of doctrine it may involve) means for me essentially his faith in the existence of an unseen order of some kind in which the riddles of the natural order may be found explained. In the more developed religions the natural world has always been regarded as the mere scaffolding or vestibule of a truer, more eternal world, and affirmed to be a sphere of education, trial, or redemption. In these religions, one must in some fashion die to the natural life before one can enter into life eternal. The notion that this physical world of wind and water, where the sun rises and the moon sets, is absolutely and ultimately the divinely aimed-at and established thing, is one which we find only in very early religions, such as that of the most primitive Jews. It is this natural religion (primitive still, in spite of the fact that poets and men of science whose good-will exceeds their perspicacity keep publishing it in new editions tuned to our contemporary ears) that, as I said a while ago, has suffered definitive bankruptcy in the opinion of a circle of persons, among whom I must count myself, and who are growing more numerous every day. For such persons the physical order of nature, taken simply as science knows it, cannot be held to reveal any one harmonious spiritual intent. It is mere *weather*, as Chauncey Wright called it, doing and undoing without end.

Now, I wish to make you feel, if I can in the short remainder of this hour, that we have a right to believe the physical order to be only a partial order; that we have a right to supplement it by an unseen spiritual order which we assume on trust, if only thereby life may seem to us better worth living again. But as such a trust will seem to some of you sadly mystical and execrably unscientific, I must first say a word or two to weaken the veto which you may consider that science opposes to our act.

There is included in human nature an ingrained naturalism and materialism of mind which can only admit facts that are actually tangible. Of this sort of mind the entity called "science" is the idol. Fondness for the word "scientist" is one of the notes by which you may know its votaries; and its short way of killing any opinion that it disbelieves in is to call it "unscientific." It must be granted that there is no slight excuse for this. Science has made such glorious leaps in the last three hundred years, and extended our knowledge of nature so enormously both in general and in detail; men of science, moreover, have as a class displayed such admirable virtues—that it is no wonder if the worshippers of science lose their head. In this very university, accordingly, I have heard more than one teacher say that all the fundamental conceptions of truth have already been found by science, and that the future has only the details of the picture to fill in. But the slightest reflection on the real conditions will suffice to show how barbaric such notions are. They show such a lack of scientific imagination, that it is hard to see how one who is actively advancing any part of science can make a mistake so crude. Think how many absolutely new scientific conceptions have arisen in our own generation, how many new problems have been formulated that were never thought of before, and then cast an eye upon the brevity of science's career. It began with Galileo, not three hundred years ago. Four thinkers since Galileo, each informing his successor of what discoveries his own lifetime had seen achieved, might have passed the torch of science into our hands as we sit here in this room. Indeed, for the matter of that, an audience much smaller than the present one, an audience of some five or six score people, if each person in it could speak for his own generation, would carry us away to the black unknown of the human species, to days without a document or monument to tell their tale. Is it credible that such a mushroom knowledge, such a growth overnight as this, *can* represent more than the minutest glimpse of what the universe will really prove to be when adequately understood? No! our science is a drop, our ignorance a sea. Whatever else be certain, this at least is certain—that the world of our present natural knowledge *is* enveloped in a larger world of *some* sort of whose residual properties we at present can frame no positive idea.

Agnostic positivism, of course, admits this principle theoretically in the most cordial terms, but insists that we must not turn it to any practical use. We have no right, this doctrine tells us, to dream dreams, or suppose anything about the unseen part of the universe, merely because to do so may be for what we are pleased to call our highest interests. We must always wait for sensible evidence for our beliefs; and where such evidence is inaccessible we must frame no hypotheses whatever. Of course this is a safe enough position *in abstracto*. If a thinker had no stake in the unknown, no vital needs, to live or languish according to what the unseen world contained, a philosophic neutrality and refusal to believe either one way or the other would be his wisest cue. But, unfortunately, neutrality is not only inwardly difficult, it is also outwardly unrealizable, where our relations to an alternative are practical and vital. This is because, as the psychologists tell us, belief and doubt are living attitudes, and involve conduct on our part. Our only way, for example, of doubting, or refusing to believe, that a certain thing *is*, is continuing to act as if it were *not*. If, for instance, I refuse to believe that the room is getting cold, I leave the windows open and light no fire just as if it still were warm. If I doubt that you are worthy of my confidence, I keep you uninformed of all my secrets just as if you were *un*worthy of the same. If I doubt the need of insuring my house, I leave it uninsured as much as if I believed there were no need. And so if I must not believe that the world is divine, I can only express that refusal by declining ever to act distinctively as if it were so, which can only mean acting on certain critical occasions as if it were *not* so, or in an irreligious way. There are, you see, inevitable occasions in life when inaction is a kind of action, and must count as action, and when not to be for is to be practically against; and in all such cases strict and consistent neutrality is an unattainable thing.

And, after all, is not this duty of neutrality where only our inner interests would lead us to believe, the most ridiculous of commands? Is it not sheer dogmatic folly to say that our inner interests can have no real connection with the forces that the hidden world may contain? In other cases divinations based on inner interests have proved prophetic enough. Take science itself! Without an imperious inner demand on our part for ideal logical and mathematical harmonies, we should never have attained to proving that such harmonies be hidden between all the chinks and interstices of the crude natural world. Hardly a law has been established in science, hardly a fact ascertained, which was not first sought after, often with sweat and blood, to gratify an inner need. Whence such needs come from we do not know; we find them in us, and biological psychology so far only classes them with Darwin's "accidental variations." But the inner need of believing that this world of nature is a sign of something more spiritual and eternal than itself is just as strong and authoritative in those who feel it, as the inner need of uniform laws of causation ever can be in a professionally scientific head. The toil of many generations has proved the latter need prophetic. Why *may* not the former one be prophetic, too? And if needs of ours outrun the visible universe, why *may* not that be a sign that an invisible universe is there? What, in short, has authority to debar us from trusting our religious demands? Science as such assuredly has no authority, for she can only say what is, not what is not; and the agnostic "thou shalt not believe without coercive sensible evidence" is simply an expression (free to anyone to make) of private personal appetite for evidence of a certain peculiar kind.

Now, when I speak of trusting our religious demands, just what do I mean by "trusting"? Is the word to carry with it license to define in detail an invisible world, and to anathematize and excommunicate those whose trust is different? Certainly not! Our faculties of belief were not primarily given us to make orthodoxies and heresies withal; they were given us to live by. And to trust our religious demands means first of all to live in the light of them, and to act as if the invisible world which they suggest were real. It is a fact of human nature, that men can live and die by the help of a sort of faith that goes without a single dogma or definition. The bare assurance that this natural order is not ultimate but a mere sign or vision, the external staging of a many-storied universe, in which spiritual forces have the last word and are eternal—this bare assurance is to such men enough to make life seem worth living in spite of every contrary presumption suggested by its circumstances on the natural plane. Destroy this inner assurance, however, vague as it is, and all the light and radiance of existence is extinguished for these persons at a stroke. Often enough the wild-eyed look at life—the suicidal mood—will then set in.

And now the application comes directly home to you and me. Probably to almost every one of us here the most adverse life would seem well worth living, if we only could be *certain* that our bravery and patience with it were terminating and eventuating and bearing fruit somewhere in an unseen spiritual world. But granting we are not certain, does it then follow that a bare trust in such a world is a fool's paradise and lubberland, or rather that it is a living attitude in which we are free to indulge? Well, we are free to trust at our own risks anything that is not impossible, and that can bring analogies to bear in its behalf. That the world of physics is probably not absolute, all the converging multitude of arguments that make in favor of idealism tend to prove; and that our whole physical life may lie soaking in a spiritual atmosphere, a dimension of being that we at present have no organ for apprehending, is vividly suggested to us by the analogy of the life of our domestic animals. Our dogs, for example, are in our human life but not of it. They witness hourly the outward body of events whose inner meaning cannot, by any possible operation, be revealed to their intelligence—events in which they themselves often play the cardinal part. My terrier bites a teasing boy, for example, and the father demands damages. The dog may be present at every step of the negotiations, and see the money paid, without an inkling of what it all means, without a suspicion that it has anything to do with *him*; and he never *can* know in his natural dog's life. Or take another case which used greatly to impress me in my medical-student days. Consider a poor dog whom they are vivisecting in a laboratory. He lies strapped on a board and shrieking at his executioners, and to his own dark consciousness is literally in a sort of hell. He cannot see a single redeeming ray in the whole business; and yet all these diabolical-seeming events are often controlled by human intentions with which, if his poor benighted mind could only be made to catch a glimpse of them, all that is heroic in him would religiously acquiesce. Healing truth, relief to future sufferings of beast and man, are to be bought by them. It may be genuinely a process of redemption. Lying on his back on the board there he may be performing a function incalculably higher than any that prosperous canine life admits of; and yet, of the whole performance, this function is the one portion that must remain absolutely beyond his ken.

Now turn from this to the life of man. In the dog's life we see the world invisible to him because we live in both worlds. In human life, although we only see our world, and his within it, yet encompassing both these worlds a still wider world may be there, as unseen by us as our world is by him; and to believe in that world *may* be the most essential function that our lives in this world have to perform. But "*may* be! *may* be!" one now hears the positivist contemptuously exclaim; "What use can a scientific life have for maybes?" Well, I reply, the "scientific" life itself has much to do with maybes, and human life at large has everything to do with them. So far as man stands for anything, and is productive or originative at all, his entire vital function may be said to have to deal with maybes. Not a victory is gained, not a deed of faithfulness or courage is done, except upon a maybe; not a service, not a sally of generosity, not a scientific exploration or experiment or textbook, that may not be a mistake. It is only by risking our persons from one hour to another that we live at all. And often enough our faith beforehand in an uncertified result *is the only thing that makes the result come true.* Suppose, for instance, that you are climbing a mountain, and have worked yourself into a position from which the only escape is by a terrible leap. Have faith that you can successfully make it, and your feet are nerved to its accomplishment. But mistrust yourself, and think of all the sweet things you have heard the scientists say of maybes, and you will hesitate so long that, at last, all unstrung and trembling, and launching yourself in a moment of despair, you roll in the abyss. In such a case (and it belongs to an enormous class), the part of wisdom as well as of courage is to *believe what is in the line of your needs,* for only by such belief is the need fulfilled. Refuse to believe, and you shall indeed be right, for you shall irretrievably perish. But believe, and again you shall be right, for you shall save yourself. You make one or the other of two possible universes true by your trust or mistrust—both universes having been only *maybes,* in this particular, before you contributed your act.

Now, it appears to me that the question whether life is worth living is subject to conditions logically much like these. It does, indeed, depend on you *the liver.* If you surrender to the nightmare view and crown the evil edifice by your own suicide, you have indeed made a picture totally black. Pessimism, completed by your act, is true beyond a doubt, so far as your world goes. Your mistrust of life has removed whatever worth your own enduring existence might have given to it; and now, throughout the whole sphere of possible influence of that existence, the mistrust has proved itself to have had divining power. But suppose, on the other hand, that instead of giving way to the nightmare view you cling to it that this world is not the *ultimatum.* Suppose you find yourself a very wellspring, as Wordsworth says, of—

> Zeal, and the virtue to exist by faith
> As soldiers live by courage; as, by strength
> Of heart, the sailor fights with roaring seas.

Suppose, however thickly evils crowd upon you, that your unconquerable subjectivity proves to be their match, and that you find a more wonderful joy than any passive pleasure can bring in trusting ever in the larger whole. Have you not now made life worth living on these terms? What sort of a thing would life really be, with your qualities ready for a tussle with it, if it only brought fair weather and gave these higher faculties of yours no scope? Please remember that optimism and pessimism are definitions of the world, and that our own reactions on the world, small as they are in bulk, are integral parts of the whole thing, and necessarily help to determine the definition. They may even be the decisive elements in determining the definition. A large mass can have its unstable equilibrium overturned by the addition of a feather's weight; a long phrase may have its sense reversed by the addition of the three letters *n-o-t*. This life is worth living, we can say, *since it is what we make it, from the moral point of view*; and we are determined to make it from that point of view, so far as we have anything to do with it, a success.

Now, in this description of faiths that verify themselves I have assumed that our faith in an invisible order is what inspires those efforts and that patience which make this visible order good for moral men. Our faith in the seen world's goodness (goodness now meaning fitness for successful moral and religious life) has verified itself by leaning on our faith in the unseen world. But will our faith in the unseen world similarly verify itself? Who knows?

Once more it is a case of *maybe*; and once more maybes are the essence of the situation. I confess that I do not see why the very existence of an invisible world may not in part depend on the personal response which any one of us may make to the religious appeal. God himself, in short, may draw vital strength and increase of very being from our fidelity. For my own part, I do not know what the sweat and blood and tragedy of this life mean, if they mean anything short of this. If this life be not a real fight, in which something is eternally gained for the universe by success, it is no better than a game of private theatricals from which one may withdraw at will. But it *feels* like a real fight—as if there were something really wild in the universe which we, with all our idealities and faithfulnesses, are needed to redeem; and first of all to redeem our own hearts from atheisms and fears. For such a half-wild, half-saved universe our nature is adapted. The deepest thing in our nature is this *Binnenleben* (as a German doctor lately has called it), this dumb region of the heart in which we dwell alone with our willingnesses and unwillingnesses, our faiths and fears. As through the cracks and crannies of caverns those waters exude from the earth's bosom which then form the fountain-heads of springs, so in these crepuscular depths of personality the sources of all our outer deeds and decisions take their rise. Here is our deepest organ of communication with the nature of things; and compared with these concrete movements of our soul all abstract statements and scientific arguments—the veto, for example, which the strict positivist pronounces upon our faith—sound to us like mere chatterings of the teeth. For here possibilities, not finished facts, are the realities with which we have actively to deal; and to quote my friend William Salter, of the Philadelphia Ethical Society, "As the essence of courage is to stake one's life on a possibility, so the essence of faith is to believe that the possibility exists."

These, then, are my last words to you: Be not afraid of life. Believe that life *is* worth living, and your belief will help create the fact. The "scientific proof" that you are right may not be clear before the day of judgment (or some stage of being which that expression may serve to symbolize) is reached. But the faithful fighters of this hour, or the beings that then and there will represent them, may then turn to the fainthearted, who here decline to go on, with words like those with which Henry IV greeted the tardy Crillon after a great victory had been gained: "Hang yourself, brave Crillon! We fought at Arques, and you were not there."

5

What Is a Full Human Life?

YOUR FRIENDLY EDITOR CONTRIBUTES thoughts on what a "full human life" might be for you.

The thoughts begin with Thomas à Kempis's extreme version of a warning you may have heard from your parents: watch out, the world is dangerous.

But steadfastly avoiding the world can lead to a kind of living death. Between the perils of embracing the world and the desiccation of dismissing it, where might you find your full human life?

DISCUSSION QUESTIONS

1. Who are one or two of your heroes? Please share.

2. How can heroes inspire us even if our own lives are so much more ordinary than theirs?

Hermits, Addicts, and Heroes

ROBERT KLITGAARD

The roles of religion and spirituality *in* society are complex and fascinating, in part because religion and spirituality are self-consciously not *of* society. They contrast the transcendental, eternal, and godly with the manifest, mortal, and all too human. The great Christian writer Thomas à Kempis prayed, typically, that "we should not seek comfort in transitory things but strive for that which is heavenly."[1]

When life is rolling along for an individual or a society, tensions between heavenly and transitory may lie dormant. Sometimes, though, there is upheaval.

A crisis occurs, and the world reveals itself as dangerous, crazy, contemptible. The things people talk about as good, the things people seek, may suddenly seem empty, even evil. So-called success. Romance. Family. Not to mention the ills of the world: cruelty, deprivation, and suffering. Our trajectory and society's may suddenly seem senseless.

Distraught, we may lurch to an extreme: renounce this dangerous, crazy, contemptible world. Ascetic strains of many religions recommend this, as Arthur Schopenhauer pointed out long ago. He theorized that an extreme avoidance of the world represented a "denial of the will to life," therefore a kind of living death.[2] His exemplars: ascetic hermits who spurned society and withdrew to their cells.

---

1. Kempis, *Imitation of Christ*, 23.

2. "Thus, it may be that the inner nature of holiness, self-renunciation, mortification of our own will, asceticism, is here [in Schopenhauer's book] for the first time expressed abstractly, and free from all mythical elements, as *denial of the will to live.* . . . He sees wherever he looks suffering humanity, the suffering brute creation, and a world that passes away. . . . Why should he now, with such knowledge of the world, assert this very

64

Upheaval and crisis may lead to a contrary conclusion: don't renounce the world but rather the restraints of religion. Those ideals we've embraced, the ways we've been taught to behave, are false prophets. Religion is the opiate of the masses. Humility is for the slave class. Reinder Ganzevoort called this reaction to crisis "a negative conversion," that is, away from religion toward society.[3] A limiting case of greedily grabbing society is the extreme addict. "In late-stage addiction . . . the desiring self largely drops out the picture, as the addicted individual begins to mindlessly consume. This impairment is clinically significant because the machinery of motivated rationality has become corrupted."[4] Addicts, too, may end up alone in a kind of cell, experiencing another kind of living death.

Hermits and addicts exist across cultures. So does a third narrative: the heroes of myth, legend, and everyday life. Here the protagonists neither avoid the world nor abuse it. Rather, heroes find in the world (and perhaps also "outside the world") their callings. They discover, or receive, big insights that make sense of contradictions in their lives and in society. And then they engage in the world and with the world, through sharing and service. They exemplify a flourishing life—and their paths can inspire us even if we are not heroes.

This article depicts these three archetypal reactions to the tensions between religion and spirituality, on the one hand, and society on the other. The results may help stimulate both academic and personal reflection.

A LIVING DEATH?

Let us return to Thomas à Kempis. Over five centuries ago, he wrote *The Imitation of Christ* as a series of teaching aides for young monks in the monastery where he resided. Its audience expanded. Indeed, *The Imitation of Christ* has been called the most widely read book in Christianity aside from the Bible.[5]

It makes for bracing reading. Thomas advises that we seek Christ in everything we do, and also that we not do many things. He warns against

---

life through constant acts of will, and thereby bind himself ever more closely to it, press it ever more firmly to himself?" Death is "most welcome, and is gladly received as a longed-for deliverance" (Schopenhauer, *World as Will*, 495, 489, 494; emphasis original).

3. Ganzevoort, "Crisis Experiences," 28.

4. Matthews, "Chronic Automaticity in Addiction," 199.

5. "Imitation of Christ," para. 2.

too many friends and too much knowledge, against women in general, and against the pleasures of the world. He recommends instead solitude, quiet, and the negation of self.

In fact, we should not just avoid the world, we should hate it. "And this is the supreme wisdom," he says, "to despise the world, and draw daily nearer to the kingdom of heaven."[6] In effect we should die now, as far as ordinary life is concerned.

> Learn now to die to the world, that you may begin to live with Christ. Learn now to despise all earthly things, that you may go freely to Christ.[7]

> [Christ speaking, through the author:] My son, you must needs be ignorant of many things: so consider yourself as dead, and crucified to the whole world.[8]

> Blessed is the man who for Your sake, Lord, bids farewell to every creature, and, forcibly overcoming his natural inclinations, crucifies the desires of the flesh by the very fervor of his spirit, in order that he may offer you pure prayer with a quiet conscience. Having excluded all worldly things from his heart and life, he will be worthy to take his place in the choir of Angels.[9]

> [Christ speaking, through the author:] And the more completely a man renounces worldly things, and the more perfectly he dies to self by the conquest of self, the sooner will grace be given.[10]

What on earth scared him so? Are there alternatives besides what Thomas advises and what Thomas fears? Are there other ways "to imitate Christ"?

Thomas was afraid of the temptations of the physical being, as opposed to the growth of the spiritual being. He believed Satan threatens everywhere, even in monasteries: at one point Thomas said that monks of many years' standing are particularly vulnerable. He feared sin, which is to him a vivid and expansive category. The temptations and sins vary greatly, and it is hard to characterize them. But let me attempt a contemporary rendition of what Thomas might have considered a fearful state of affairs.

6. Kempis, *Imitation of Christ*, 27–28.
7. Kempis, *Imitation of Christ*, 59.
8. Kempis, *Imitation of Christ*, 150.
9. Kempis, *Imitation of Christ*, 158–59.
10. Kempis, *Imitation of Christ*, 212.

Suppose our inclination is not to avoid life but to embrace it. We want to experience the best of this world. Suppose further that we discover that many of the high points of life are the products of *pleasure, status, and power.* Suppose we therefore design our lives to attain pleasure, status, and power. Many of the pleasures are a function of money, so we seek money. Status and power come in part from factors that we can't help, such as gender and race and age and innate endowments, and also from things we can help at least in part, such as education, style, and career. And so, we pursue money, and we choose our education, style, and jobs to enhance our status and power.

This is a stark and unflattering characterization; let us now take it to extremes.[11]

For many people, among the most extreme of *pleasures* are intoxication, sexual union, and what might be called personal magic. The last means the feeling you have when, for example, you solve a difficult problem, play a beautiful piece of music, make a splendid soufflé, win a big tennis match, or otherwise display your own special style and relationships. John Updike writes:

Perfection Wasted

And another regrettable thing about death
is the ceasing of your own brand of magic,
which took a whole life to develop and market—
the quips, the witticisms, the slant
adjusted to a few, those loved ones nearest
the lip of the stage, their soft faces blanched
in the footlight glow, their laughter close to tears,
their tears confused with their diamond earrings,
their warm pooled breath in and out with your heartbeat,
their response and your performance twinned.

---

11. Emil Brunner described a version of intoxication with the world: "The natural 'inclination' of our heart and will is to seek ourselves. Like the rapacious spider that sits in the center of his web, we sit in the midst of our world in a spirit of acquisitiveness. We want men and what men have, their happiness, their possessions, their honor, their power. All this is our booty. But we want also from men their love, their respect, their time, and their sympathy. Our Ego sits like a king enthroned and demands that the world serve it. My wife, my children, my school, and—yes, even my dear God, are all to serve 'me.' *I* am the Lord my God. Some maintain the primacy of the ego with delicacy, others coarsely; but all maintain it. So is the natural man, the unconverted man, the godless, loveless man. If any believes that I have made too harsh a judgment let him speak for himself. I confess in any case that *I* am such a man—and those I know are such people" (Brunner, *Our Faith*, 99–100; emphasis original).

The jokes over the phone. The memories packed
in the rapid-access file. The whole act.
Who will do it again? That's it: no one;
imitators and descendants aren't the same.

For many people, among the most extreme experiences of *status and power* are access to exclusive benefits and the power to make decisions that others will or must follow. Arguably, today's world contains more opportunities for pleasures such as intoxication, sexual union, and personal magic than most people could enjoy at most times in history. Arguably, the average person today has more access than ever before to important places and decisions that in the past were restricted to a privileged few.

If so, would people today be experiencing greater levels of happiness and fulfillment and joy than in centuries past? Would people start to have "enough" of these pleasures and "enough" status and power so that they would seek "something more"?

I think the answer to both questions may be no, at least for many people. In this sense Thomas à Kempis had a point. Imagine Thomas stating, "I do not believe that people are on average better off with greater access to alcohol and drugs than with less, with greater sexual freedom than with less, and with greater opportunities to display their personal magic, because all these things lead people away from God." Thomas was also skeptical of what happens to people who focus on status and power, and so he advocated the polar opposites: humility and obedience.

The extremes Thomas feared may include these.

- Drug addicts so intoxicated with intoxication that they end up with bad health, confusion, and a decreasing ability to experience real pleasure

- Sexually promiscuous people so dedicated to conquests and orgasms that sexual union becomes jaded and unsatisfying

- People so dedicated to their personal magic that they become less interested in the magic for its own sake and more interested in how they compare with other people and their personal magics—in which case, the magic can disappear

In these extreme cases, we perceive the opposite of Thomas's own recommended escape from society. But may we note a similarity? Does the extreme drug addict also experience a kind of living death? Not like

Thomas's hermetical monk, which Schopenhauer praised as a noble and virtuous example of will, a spiritually motivated withdrawal from society that may end up closer to Being. But an extreme addict, who moves from dose to dose in a semiconscious stupor, with the "highs" less and less like those moments of joy the addict originally sought, may also end up alone in his cell, also far away from a flourishing life.

THE OPPOSITE OF A LIVING DEATH

A flourishing life? What does that mean? Let's work toward it from the two extremes of living deaths—from the side of Thomas's ideal monk and from the side of the extreme addict. And let's leave behind the term "monk" for the more secular term "hermit," acknowledging that not all monks are hermits,[12] not all hermits are religious or spiritual, and indeed some hermits are addicts (of the Internet, for example).[13]

Consider the characterization of figure 1. From the hermit, let us move upward on the left to religious people trying to make their ways and avoid sin.

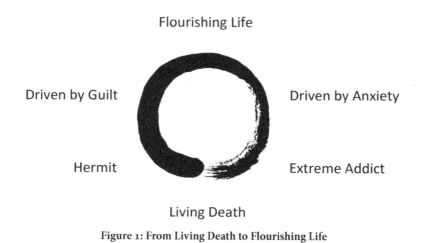

Figure 1: From Living Death to Flourishing Life

Friedrich Nietzsche disparaged people whose ultimate goal is to avoid guilt. "Now I know what people sought formerly above all else when they

12. Monks come in many varieties, including many such as the Taizé community who engage fully with people outside their monasteries (Moorhouse, *Beyond All Reasons*).

13. Stip et al., "Internet Addiction."

sought teachers of virtue. Good sleep they sought for themselves, and pop-py-head virtues to promote it."[14] A good night's sleep as the ultimate goal: by this he meant people whose objectives are to feel no guilt, to be materi-ally secure, to wall off a little world of peace and quiet. Nothing is wrong with these three goals per se; Nietzsche criticized making them the purpose of one's life. He deplored people for whom the avoidance of guilty feelings becomes the ultimate objective, for whom comfort becomes the blessed state, for whom peace towers over all other states of the world. In making these desirable feelings ultimate aims, such people may seem to us as well as to Nietzsche to be missing something more important in a flourishing life. I leave this as a thought to return to in a moment.

Now start from the other limiting case, the extreme addict. From there, let us move upward to a materialistic, pleasure- and status-seeking person who is not, however, a self-destructive addict. Think of people dedicated to surface pleasures and signs of status and power, preoccupied with how well they are doing compared with someone else or with socially instigated styles or standards of living. Their daily worries are about things that even they, in moments of reflection, may admit are superficial signs of "success." They are characterized by anxiety rather than guilt, by a concern for relative status rather than absolute security. They make the avoidance of anxiety and the achievement of status the ultimate aims—and find that these are unattainable because there is always one more thing to buy, one more rung to climb, one more task left undone.

What is at the top of the circle? What ideal of a flourishing life is the opposite of both kinds of living death?

HEROES

Across many cultures, one finds myths and examples of heroes. What "hero" means varies, and the details of heroic lives are diverse.[15] And yet, patterns have been discerned. The Greek epic hero, said the classicist Gregory Nagy, is characterized by three elements:

14. Nietzsche, *Thus Spake Zarathustra*, 16.

15. "The words 'epic' and 'hero' both defy generalization, let alone universalizing definitions," states Gregory Nagy in the first sentence of "The Epic Hero." The great medieval scholar Ernst Curtius concludes, "A comparative phenomenology of heroism, heroic poetry, and the heroic ideal is yet to be given us" (*European Literature*, 170). Paul Johnson points out that the heroes of one era may be pariahs in another, for example, British colonial conquerors (*Heroes*).

1. The hero is unseasonal.

2. The hero is extreme—positively (for example, "best" in whichever category) or negatively (the negative aspect can be a function of the hero's unseasonality).

3. The hero is antagonistic toward the god who seems to be most like the hero; antagonism does not rule out an element of attraction—often a "fatal attraction"—which is played out in a variety of ways.[16]

By "unseasonal," Nagy meant outside the usual pattern of life. Heroes leave the usual path or cycle. And this being out of season prods them, indeed enables them, to be heroic.[17]

In Europe in the late Middle Ages,

> the hero is the ideal personal type whose being is centered upon nobility and its realization—hence upon "pure" not technical, values—and whose basic virtue is natural nobility in body and soul. The hero is distinguished by a superabundance of intellectual will and by its concentration against the instincts. It is this which characterizes his greatness of character. The specific virtue of the hero is self-control. But the hero's will does not rest here, it presses into power, responsibility, daring.[18]

16. Nagy, *Ancient Greek Hero*, 1.50.

17. "The goddess of being on time [Hērā] makes sure that the hero [Hēraklēs or Hercules] should start off his lifespan by *being not on time* and that he should go through life by trying to catch up—and never quite managing to do so until the very end. . . . And yet, without this unseasonality, without the disequilibrium brought about by the persecution of Hērā, Hēraklēs would never have achieved the equilibrium of immortality and the kleos or 'glory' that makes his achievements live forever in song" (Nagy, *Ancient Greek Hero*, 1.45, 1.49).

18. Curtius, *European Literature*, 167.

And one can compare the Shakespearean hero,[19] the hero of nineteenth-century Romanticism,[20] and "the hero of history."[21]

Amid this variety, Joseph Campbell identified common features.[22] Their life journeys feature momentous departures that often involve a calling, some sort of initiation including a realization about themselves and their place in the world, and a return home.

In this article, we play with a simplification of this sequence.

- Heroes experience a *calling*.

- They attain a big *insight* about themselves and the world.

- And then they *share and serve*.

It is not just mythological heroes who portray this pattern. David Bornstein studied people around the world who work at the grassroots level and make a difference. He noted that each of them had a hero, someone close to them with "outstandingly strong values." And at some point in their lives, a combination of a crucial event and their own preparation yielded a conversion experience that in turn led to a life of sharing and serving.

> However the influences differ, a pattern remains: At some moment in their lives, social entrepreneurs get it into their heads that it is up to them to solve a particular problem. Usually something has

19. "The hero, with Shakespeare, is a person of high degree of public importance, and that his actions or sufferings are of an unusual kind. But this is not all. His nature also is exceptional" (Bradley, *Shakespearean Tragedy*, 20). Bradley added the classic feature of the tragic hero in Shakespeare: "In the circumstances where we see the hero placed, his tragic trait, which is also his greatness, is fatal to him" (21).

20. "He has to be made of pure gold; he has to be kind and dedicated, to suffer a trial by ordeal—loneliness and all that—and he must, absolutely must, be a man of genius. There are two strong reasons why the young rebel must be so outstanding. First, his excellence resolves the conflict between the conservatism and the progressivism within the romantic philosophy: the rebel is a progressive force, but he must be idolized, in order that there will be no widespread attempt to emulate him: the greatest majority are followers, and only a few can be leaders. Second, only the most excellent can transcend the tradition, yet thereby enrich it rather than destroy it" (Agassi, "Genius in Science," 151).

21. The philosopher Sidney Hook studied examples in literature, music, and painting; philosophy and science; religion; and "the historical hero." To Hook, the hero is not just an eventful person but an event-making person "whose actions are the consequences of outstanding capacities of intelligence, will, and character rather than of accidents of position. . . . [A] hero is great not merely in virtue of what he does but in virtue of what he is" (*Hero in History*, 99–100).

22. Campbell, "Hero with Thousand Faces."

been brewing inside for a long time, and at a particular moment in time—often triggered by an event—personal preparedness, social need, and historical opportunity converge and the person takes decision action. The word "decision" comes from the Latin *decidere*, meaning "to cut off." From that point on, the social entrepreneurs seem to cut off other options for themselves.[23]

Such examples can help us appreciate a flourishing life. Even if we cannot agree on the meaning of life, the philosopher Tim Mawson points out that "a life, a period or an aspect within a life, or even an individual action within a life is said to be more deeply meaningful than another and there is a notable consensus on such first-order judgments, a consensus that spans very different theories of what the meaning of life is."[24] We may then note that many examples of flourishing lives contain common features: calling, insight, and then sharing and service.[25]

CALLING

The psychologist Abraham H. Maslow studied "self-actualizing people," his term for the "more matured, more fully human" among us. Their basic needs of belongingness, affection, respect, and self-esteem are gratified. They are spontaneous, natural, "more easily themselves than other people." What characterizes these people?

> Self-actualizing people are, without one single exception, involved in something outside of themselves. They are devoted, working at something, something which is very precious to them—some calling or vocation in the old sense, the priestly sense. They are working at something which fate has called them to and which they work hard at and which they love, so that the work-joy dichotomy in them disappears.[26]

23. Bornstein, *How to Change the World*, 240.

24. Mawson, *God and the Meanings*, 16.

25. In a different vein, psychologists have studied how (predominantly American) respondents define heroes and their characteristics. One recent list of heroic attributes: bravery, moral integrity, conviction, courageous, self-sacrifice, protecting, honesty, selfless, determined, saves others, inspiring, and helpful. Less common but frequently included: proactive, humble, strong, risk-taker, fearless, caring, powerful, compassionate, leadership skills, exceptional, intelligent, talented, and personable (Kinsella et al., "Zeroing In on Heroes").

26. Maslow, *Farther Reaches*, 43.

What does it mean to have a calling? "The best way to communicate these feelings to someone who doesn't intuitively, directly understand them is to use as a model 'falling in love.' This is clearly different from doing one's duty, or doing what is sensible and logical."[27]

The psychologists Jeanne Nakamura and Mihaly Csikszentmihalyi interviewed hundreds of successful painters, dancers, poets, novelists, physicists, biologists, and psychologists—all people who seem to have crafted lives for themselves built around a consuming passion. These are admirable lives, the sort that many young people dream of having. The authors wanted to know how such lives happened.

Amid all their idiosyncrasies, these people shared what Nakamura and Csikszentmihalyi called "vital engagement," which "is characterized by completeness of involvement or participation and marked by intensity. There is a strong felt connection between self and object; a writer is 'swept away' by a project, a scientist is 'mesmerized by the stars.' The relationship has subjective meaning; work is a 'calling.'"[28]

INSIGHT

Like a calling, an *insight* also creates an "aha," but now of a more cognitive sort. A big insight makes sense of things that heretofore were mysterious or contradictory or unconnected. A big insight clarifies the world, not just one's own situation and challenges.[29]

Sometimes the calling or the insight, or perhaps both, originate with what Maslow called a "peak experience." Almost all his self-actualizing subjects had therapeutic effects from peak experiences described as "mystic" or "oceanic" or "a cognition of being." Their insights were "so profound as to remove neurotic symptoms forever; or were followed by greater creativity, spontaneity, or expressiveness; or produced a more or less permanently changed, more healthy world-view, and so on."[30]

The hero of Hermann Hesse's *The Glass Bead Game* described his peak experiences as glimpses of reality.

---

27. Maslow, *Farther Reaches*, 301.
28. Nakamura and Csikszentmihalyi, "Construction of Meaning," 86.
29. Klitgaard, "From Insight to Ideology."
30. Maslow, *Psychology of Being*, 95.

What gives these experiences their weight and persuasiveness is not their truth, their sublime origin, their divinity or anything of the sort, but their reality. They are tremendously real, somewhat in the way a violent physical pain or a surprising natural event, a storm or an earthquake, seem to us charged with an entirely different sort of reality, presence, inexorability, from ordinary times and conditions. . . . Later on we may start to question them or examine their significance, if that is our bent; but at the moment they admit no doubts and are brimful of reality. My "awakening" has a similar kind of intensified reality for me.[31]

Insights may arrive unexpectedly and from a humble source. The psychologist Martin Seligman was one of those who discovered that people could willfully become more grateful and optimistic and therefore happier and healthier. But he struggled to apply the insight to himself. It took his five-year-old daughter Nikki to generate his conversion experience.

One day, Seligman and Nikki were weeding in the garden.

I have to confess that even though I have written a book and many articles about children, I'm actually not very good with them. I am goal-oriented and time-urgent and when I'm weeding in the garden, I'm weeding. Nikki, however, was throwing weeds into the air and dancing and singing. Since she was distracting me, I yelled at her, and she walked away. Within a few minutes, she was back, saying, "Daddy, I want to talk to you."

"Yes, Nikki?"

"Daddy, do you remember before my fifth birthday? From when I was three until when I was five, I was a whiner. I whined every day. On my fifth birthday, I decided I wasn't going to whine any more.

"That was the hardest thing I've ever done. And if I can stop whining, you can stop being such a grouch."

This was an epiphany for me. In terms of my own life, Nikki hit the nail right on the head. I was a grouch. I had spent fifty years enduring mostly wet weather in my soul, and the last ten years as a walking nimbus cloud in a household radiant with sunshine. Any good fortune I had was probably not due to being grumpy, but in spite of it. In that moment, I resolved to change.[32]

31. Hesse, *Glass Bead Game*, 395.
32. Seligman, *Authentic Happiness*, 28.

Margaret Mead describes how insight can occur unexpectedly in a conference. Note her characterizations of receiving a big insight: something akin to a conversion, something like falling in love, an aesthetic experience.

> Sometimes a conference experience is given enormously heightened intensity through the dissolution of barriers due to hierarchy or formal professional rivalry, race or class prejudice, or simple cross-disciplinary ignorance. When this happens, something akin to a conversion may occur. For other participants, the experience may have some of the quality of heightened perception that comes from falling in love. Those with eidetic imagery may fall asleep with the faces of every member etched on their eyeballs or the voices of each ringing in their ears. For others the emergence of a new conceptualization may be primarily an aesthetic experience.[33]

SHARING AND SERVING

In the heroic progression, *sharing and serving* come next. The calling and the insight are not confined to the hero's own well-being or sanctification. They are imparted.

What does *sharing* a calling and an insight mean? It is probably not the same as teaching a scientific theory or demonstrating a chemical reaction. This kind of sharing is usually done artistically, through metaphor and myth, parable and philosophical abstraction, and/or through a practical program of discipline and passion combined.

And *serving* is part of the equation. The service is often directed toward causes and people that those driven by anxiety and guilt wish to avoid and exclude. The hero serves the needy and the forgotten, even the sinners and the enemies of society.

Sharing and serving, to be done well, must be attentive to situation, norms, and conventions. Sharing and serving have to be tailored to individuals as well—to a person's feelings, needs, fears, and level of preparation. As a hypothesis, I would suggest that sharing and serving should presuppose a relationship. The relationship could be one of community, or it could be one of friendship or love.

Imagine you and I are lucky enough to receive sharing and service from other people. If those people are dour and impersonal, if we feel that they are simply doing a duty or worse a penance, we will not be happy even

33. Mead and Byers, *Small Conference*, 40.

though we may be appreciative. But if those people share with us and serve us with kindness and joy, as if they want to share and serve for the delight it gives them, then we will receive them very differently. Anne Colby and William Damon studied "moral exemplars" who served others in remarkable, sustained ways. What they had in common was

> strong, enduring, and general *positivity* toward their lives, toward their work, and toward other people. What do we mean by "positivity"? First, we are referring to an enjoyment of life, especially an enjoyment of the work they are doing—whether it is fighting for racial justice, helping the poor, or working for peace.[34]

Also, these moral exemplars exhibited a sense of humor, humility, and "the ability to see oneself as contributing to an ongoing effort, not a savior who is out to change the world."[35] "The true knight of faith," Søren Kierkegaard admonished, "is a witness, never a teacher, and therein lies his deep humanity, which is worth a great deal more than this silly participation in others' weal and woe which is honored by the name of sympathy, whereas in fact it is nothing but vanity."[36]

And finally, we should be suspicious of characterizing ourselves as the Givers and others as Takers. John Steinbeck wrote a remarkable essay about his friend Ed Ricketts, the unorthodox scientist and local legend who was the model for the character of Doc in *Cannery Row*. After Ed's death, Steinbeck tried to analyze "the great talent that was in Ed Ricketts, that made him so loved and needed and makes him so missed now that he is dead." Steinbeck eventually decided that Ed's talent lay in

> his ability to receive, to receive anything from anyone, to receive gratefully and thankfully and make the gift seem very fine. Because of this everyone felt good in giving to Ed—a present, a thought, anything.
>
> Perhaps the most overrated virtue on our list of shoddy virtues is that of giving. Giving builds up the ego of the giver, makes him superior and higher and larger than the receiver. Nearly always, giving is a selfish pleasure, and in many cases it is downright destructive and evil thing. One has only to remember some of our wolfish financiers who spend two-thirds of their lives clawing fortunes out of the guts of society and the latter third pushing it

34. Colby and Damon, *Some Do Care*, 262.

35. Colby and Damon, *Some Do Care*, 272.

36. Kierkegaard, *Fear and Trembling*, 90.

back. It is not enough to suppose that their philanthropy is a kind of frightened restitution, or that their natures change when they have enough. Such a nature never has enough and natures do not change that readily. I think the impulse is the same in both cases. For giving can bring the same sense of superiority as getting does, and philanthropy may be another kind of spiritual avarice.

It is so easy to give, so exquisitely rewarding. Receiving, on the other hand, if it be well done, requires a fine balance of self-knowledge and kindness. It requires humility and tact and great understanding of relationships. In receiving you cannot appear, even to yourself, better or stronger or wiser than the giver, although you must be wiser to do it well.[37]

Note a parallel comment by Kierkegaard: "He had not even comprehended the little mystery, that it is better to give than to receive, and has no inkling of the great one, that it is far more difficult to receive than to give."[38]

THE HERO'S EXAMPLE OF FLOURISHING LIFE

When our world is in upheaval, we may recoil to extremes.

We may renounce the world.

Or we may grab the world, renouncing every limit on our grabbing.

As the poet Lisa Wells notes, "When a person has a problem with numbing or checking out, violence, drunkenness, sex, hallucination, whatever—extremes can be very seductive, as a strategy to feel and to locate a boundary."[39]

Wells's book *Believers* is about people who avoid these extremes, "people who have suffered painful traumas and have found ways to reconcile with that history, and now devote their lives to bringing reconciliation into the world. There's no abstraction, there's nothing really—and I don't mean for this to sound anti-intellectual—but there's nothing really academic about it. It's like, 'I survived and therefore I will help others.'"[40]

We have called these three reactions to upheaval the hermit, the addict, and the hero. So far apart, the hermit and the addict. And yet, possibly

---

37. Steinbeck, *Sea of Cortez*, lxiv–lxv.

38. Kierkegaard, *Fear and Trembling*, 113.

39. Juliani, "Lisa Wells," final para.

40. Juliani, "Lisa Wells," para. 36.

similar in this way: they both may end up alone, removed from society, experiencing a kind of living death.

Hermits and addicts, with different names, appear in every culture, every epoch. So does the hero. Unlike the hermit and the addict, heroes are engaged with the world, in spades. Full of a calling that matters for its own sake. Grateful for a big insight that connects a kind of existential problem they face intimately with a social problem that affects many. And then, with their callings in heart and insights in mind, heroes don't withdraw in satisfaction or self-glorification. They share and serve, through their work and by their example. With a combination of boldness and humility, they reach for the impossible.[41]

Heroes are, in cultural manifestations, rare beings. But there are also on-the-ground humble heroes.[42] They are not demigods or Shakespearean protagonists. They are not John Keats suffering through a cold night, alone, writing poetry. Nor the beleaguered Great Leader, in the office long after others have gone home. Rather, these everyday heroes are smiling, dedicated, engaged, assured. "It is a picture of striking joy, great certainty, and unremitting faith; one that results in both high standards for the self and charity toward others."[43]

"It is not so much that they overcome their fears, doubts, or resentments over the risks and hardships in their lives; it is more that they treasure the chance to take them on. The exemplars create for themselves a world of certainty rather than doubt, a perspective of faith rather than despair."[44]

These heroes introduce an image of religion and spirituality in society that is quite different from that of Thomas à Kempis.[45] It is also far

41. Max Weber observed: "It takes both passion and perspective. Certainly all historical experience confirms the truth—that man would not have attained the possible unless time and again he had reached out for the impossible. But to do that a man must be a leader, and not only a leader but a hero as well, in a very sober sense of the word. And even those who are neither leaders nor heroes must arm themselves with that steadfastness of heart which can brave even the crumbling of all hopes" ("Politics as a Vocation," 128).

42. Worthington and Allison, *Heroic Humility*.

43. Colby and Damon, *Some Do Care*, 5.

44. Colby and Damon, *Some Do Care*, xii.

45. Thanks to Jesus P. Estanislao for showing me the relevance of Josemaría Escrivá's concepts and implementation of religion and spirituality in everyday life, and to Thomas Glenn Jackson III for introducing me to E. Stanley Jones's evangelical Protestant version of many consonant ideas. Coincidentally, both Escrivá and Jones wrote devotional books with the title *The Way*—and they both recommended conveying Christian callings and

away from lives that concentrate on pleasure and status, or on security and peace. It transcends selfish conceptions of the ultimate good. It accepts the wonder of an individual calling and reveres the possibility of a deeply felt and transforming insight. It addresses, indeed embraces, the imperfections of this world.

insights through humble and heroic sharing and serving.

Excerpt from *Prevail*

ROBERT KLITGAARD

WHICH HERO?

If we have experienced a sense of rightness in a hero's saga, the hero may become our own source of strength. We may have faith in the power of that example to transform our lives and through us, we hope, the lives of others. With their stories close to our hearts, we can become more heroic—even if we are in no grand sense "heroes"—in our mundane lives.

An artistic analogy is useful. Our appreciation of beauty may in some sense hinge upon those especially gifted and experienced to create it. "The spirit of an artist's gifts can wake our own," notes Lewis Hyde. "We may not have the power to profess our gifts as the artist does, and yet we come to recognize, and in a sense to receive, the endowments of our being through the agency of his creation."[1]

In the same way, people vary in their abilities to find a calling, discover an insight, and live both calling and insight through sharing and serving. In our diversity, those of us who have less ability and experience may well find inspiration and instruction from those with more. "It is very similar in the domain of the religious consciousness, religious production, and revelation," Rudolph Otto wrote. "Here, too, most men have only the 'predisposition,' in the sense of a receptiveness and susceptibility to religion and a capacity for freely recognizing and judging religious truth at first hand. . . . The prophet [or we might say, the hero] corresponds in the religious sphere to the creative artist in that of art: he is the man in whom the Spirit shows

---

1. Hyde, *Gift*, xvii.

itself alike as the power to hear 'the voice within' and the power of divination, and in each case appears as a creative force."[2]

One question is how to identify heroes whose sagas are meaningful *for us*. Ideally, we would have heroes whose callings inspire us, whose insights speak to own very personal dilemmas, and who informs our all-too-human dilemma of sharing and serving as imperfect beings. Heroes who would help us see that it is the purity of our love that matters, not how gifted we are in love or how powerful we are so that our love has a wider radius. Ideally, we would feel it is all right for us to be imperfect in execution, all right to be a human being, all right to be confused about what to do and how—provided we are aligned with our calling and feel it in our hearts. Learning from these heroes, we would understand that a flourishing life is open to nonheroes, too, just like us.

HEROISM IN THE LARGE AND THE SMALL

Heroic examples inspire us, in literature and legend, history and religion, and also in the real world around us, because their lives are works of art that matter to us.

What is the antithesis of a work of art? Many things, I'm sure, but let me highlight one category: the cliché, the adage, the recipe. Big insights are poorly conveyed by maxims, as Thomas Macaulay noted long ago:

> Every man who has seen the world knows that nothing is so useless as a general maxim. If it be very moral and very true, it may serve for a copy to a charity-boy. If, like those of Rochefoucault, it be sparkling and whimsical, it may make an excellent motto for an essay. But few indeed of the many wise apophthegms which have been uttered, from the time of the Seven Sages to that of Poor Richard, have prevented a single foolish action.[3]

A heroic life is rarely discovered or conveyed through a recipe or a plan. It may be imagined or experienced through art, or by being (or trying to be) yourself a work of art. "It is the purity of our effort in love that matters, not our prowess or the radius of our talents and influence. When we receive the gift of love, we feel deep down that it is all right for us to be imperfect, all right to be human beings, all right to be confused about what to

---

2. Otto, *Idea of the Holy*, 177–78.
3. Macaulay, *Poetry and Prose*, 263.

do and how."[4] So, too, with how you face your upheavals, make big choices, and tentatively progress down your own heroic path. If your trying is pure, this may itself be sufficient for artistic and therefore for human success; let us leave that as a point for reflection.

We should share and serve, not just in the abstract or for a cause, but through and because of relationships such as friendships and communities, marriage and family. Heroism shows up in the interstices of life. One section of St. Josemaría Escrivá's book *The Way* is entitled "Little Things." Here are two of Escrivá's observations:

> 823 Have you noticed how human love consists of little things? Well, divine love also consists of little things.

> 813 Do everything for love. In that way there will be no little things: everything will be big. Perseverance in the little things for love is heroism.

One finds similar ideas in Mahayana Buddhism. Their human heroes, the Bodhisattvas, devote themselves to the service of others. "Liberating or saving those who were lost or suffering becomes the sole life purpose of those who take this Bodhisattva vow, even today," notes Charley Linden Thorp.[5] Before departing from the world, the Buddha declared that everyone, including women, could become enlightened, not just monks. Especially in Mahayana Buddhism, enlightenment went beyond the individual ascetic in solitary seeking; it included, indeed emphasized, sharing and serving. "It might be said," writes Thorp, "that for a long period of time monks remained cloistered hearing the Dharma, while the laity were actively working as Bodhisattvas in daily life."[6] Like the Bodhisattvas, we can aspire to bring our calling, our insights, and our compassionate desire to share and serve into every little thing we do.

YOUR LIFE, YOUR HERO

For you, what would be the characteristics of particularly promising heroes? Given all that we have considered so far, let us conclude with some suggestions.

---

4. Klitgaard, *Prevail*, 105.
5. Thorp, "Mahayana Buddhism," para. 20.
6. Thorp, "Mahayana Buddhism," para. 23.

The heroes would have received and would themselves issue a calling. Their calling would resonate with you. Ideally, the calling would speak to you in your unique situation, *and* you would recognize the calling as embracing others, equally unique.

The heroes would have received insights that you can in turn receive through them, so to speak aesthetically and especially through their lives as works of art. The heroes' upheavals and big decisions would inspire you as you face your own. The heroes' messages would help you with challenges in the large and in the small.

You might receive from them a calling that feels something like falling in love and a big insight that makes you say, "Aha!"

Like many deep insights, the insights you gain from these heroes might appear obvious once you have them, but paradoxical to those who didn't have them. You would also find that there are processes for conveying the insight with some but not complete success—not everyone gets it, even when they try. But the insight itself would not exclude anyone from possessing it. The insight is not equal to a formula or maxim, even if you might later use a formula to remind yourself.

The heroes would share their callings and insights with people like you and me specifically, as individuals. The way they serve, the why of their sacrifice, would exemplify love.

Finally, your ideal heroes would confront inside their lives a contradiction or dilemma that also inhabits the world outside. The grander the dilemmas, and the more you recognize them and empathize with them and are astonished by them, the greater the hero's resonance and relevance will be.

PART II

INTRODUCING JESUS

6

What Is Special about Jesus?

ADAM GOPNIK IS ONE of America's leading writers and critics. Trained in fine arts, his remarkable range of accomplishment spans politics, literature, cuisine, fantasy novels, writing musicals . . . and writing about what it all means.

On his mother's side, a long line of rabbis. His father, a nonbelieving Jew. His wife, a Lutheran. His formative Christian exposure: Christmas.

> My parents, by the standard turns and twists of generations, rejected the religious content of their own upbringing. So one of the strange things in my upbringing was that we celebrated Christmas with enormous intensity, because—it's a long and complicated story—one of my mother's relatives was actually Irish Catholic. And most of my early—I don't know how to call it, exactly—spiritual experiences derived from this very strange, and yet hardly idiosyncratic, because it's actually quite widespread—experience of a Jewish Christmas. . . .
>
> One of the things that came to be hugely important to me was— one of the portals of my own experience of the numinous, the spiritual, call it what you will—was Christmas music: the Bach *Christmas Oratorio*, Handel's *Messiah*, medieval carols, which ultimately then led me to the great Christian poetry of that time.[7]

7. Tippett, "Adam Gopnik," paras. 7–8.

But I think in our time, those of us who grow up in doubt, who accept scientific skepticism as a foundational part of our worldview, also are drawn again and again to kinds of faith, to spiritual practice.[8]

At Christmas church services, Gopnik said he's the one in the back pew blubbering away.[9]

His 2023 book *The Real Work: On the Mystery of Mastery* distinguishes *achievement*, which he calls spiritually empty, from *accomplishment*, "that moment of mastery when suddenly we feel that something profoundly difficult, tenaciously thorny, has given way." We can study masters to see how they attained it. Even better, he recommends, we can ourselves experiment with acquiring mastery in a variety of areas small and perhaps large. "I came to see, in drawing as much as in boxing and dancing, that we miss the whole if we don't attempt to grasp, in however limited and even feeble a form, what the real work feels like for other people as they do it."[10]

This message may recall a theme in our last two chapters: we find meaning in our lives not by adopting certainties nor by giving up, but by trying things out despite all our maybes: by experimenting with our lives. For example, this quote from William James:

> So far as man stands for anything, and is productive or originative at all, his entire vital function may be said to have to deal with maybes. Not a victory is gained, not a deed of faithfulness or courage is done, except upon a maybe; not a service, not a sally of generosity, not a scientific exploration or experiment or textbook, that may not be a mistake. It is only by risking our persons from one hour to another that we live at all. And often enough our faith beforehand in an uncertified result *is the only thing that makes the result come true.*[11]

In this chapter, Gopnik brilliantly reviews recent scholarly literature about Jesus to discern, amid all the puzzles and contradictions, what makes Jesus uncanny and unique.

8. Tippett, "Adam Gopnik," para. 42.
9. Tippett, "Adam Gopnik," para. 60.
10. Gopnik, *Real Work*, 2.
11. James, "Is Life Worth Living," this vol., 59–60; emphasis original.

DISCUSSION QUESTIONS

1. Gopnik writes: "Jesus' morality has a brash, sidewise indifference to conventional ideas of goodness. . . . There is a wild gaiety about Jesus' moral teachings that still leaps off the page. He is informal in a new way, too, that remains unusual among prophets."[12]

   What examples of these things in Gopnik's essay impressed you? How do they belie stereotypes about religion?

2. Read aloud these sentences of Gopnik's:

   > Certain kinds of truths are convincing only in a narrative. . . . If God he was—not some Hindu-ish avatar or offspring of God, but actually one with God—then God once was born and had dirty diapers and took naps. The longer you think about it, the more astounding, or absurd, it becomes. To be really believed at all, it can only be told again. . . .
   >
   > If one thing seems clear from all the scholarship, though, it's that Paul's divine Christ came first, and Jesus the wise rabbi came later. This fixed, steady twoness at the heart of the Christian story can't be wished away by liberal hope any more than it could be resolved by theological hair-splitting. Its intractability is part of the intoxication of belief. It can be amputated, mystically married, revealed as a fraud, or worshipped as the greatest of mysteries. The two go on, and their twoness is what distinguishes the faith and gives it its discursive dynamism.[13]

   a. What is the "fixed, steady twoness" of the Christian story?

   b. What do you think Gopnik means by "the intoxication of belief"?

   c. If this twoness cannot be wished away or intellectually resolved, what do you think it means that some things can only be believed by telling them again, like stories?

---

12. Gopnik, "What Did Jesus Do," this vol., 95.

13. Gopnik, "What Did Jesus Do," this vol., 97, 99.

What Did Jesus Do?

ADAM GOPNIK

When we meet Jesus of Nazareth at the beginning of the Gospel of Mark, almost surely the oldest of the four, he's a full-grown man. He comes down from Galilee, meets John, an ascetic desert hermit who lives on locusts and wild honey, and is baptized by him in the River Jordan. If one thing seems nearly certain to the people who read and study the Gospels for a living, it's that this really happened: John the Baptizer—as some like to call him, to give a better sense of the original Greek's flat-footed active form—baptized Jesus. They believe it because it seems so unlikely, so at odds with the idea that Jesus always played the star in his own show: why would anyone have said it if it weren't true? This curious criterion governs historical criticism of Gospel texts: the more improbable or "difficult" an episode or remark is, the likelier it is to be a true record, on the assumption that you would edit out all the weird stuff if you could, and keep it in only because the tradition is so strong that it can't plausibly be excluded. If Jesus says something nice, then someone is probably saying it for him; if he says something nasty, then probably he really did.

So then, the scholars argue, the author of Mark, whoever he was—the familiar names conventionally attached to each Gospel come later—added the famous statement of divine favor, descending directly from the heavens as they opened. But what does the voice say? In Mark, the voice says, "You are my Son, whom I love; with you I am well pleased," seeming to inform a Jesus who doesn't yet know that this is so. But some early versions of Luke have the voice quoting Psalm 2: "You are my Son; today I have begotten you." Only in Matthew does it announce Jesus' divinity to the world as though it were an ancient, fixed agreement, not a new act. In Mark, for that matter, the two miraculous engines that push the story forward at the

start and pull it toward heaven at the end—the virgin birth and the resurrection—make no appearance at all. The story begins with Jesus' adult
baptism, with no hint of a special circumstance at his birth, and there is
actually some grumbling by Jesus about his family ("Only in his hometown,
among his relatives and in his own house, is a prophet without honor," he
complains); it ends with a cry of desolation as he is executed—and then an
enigmatic and empty tomb. (It's left to the Roman centurion to recognize
him as the Son of God after he is dead, while the verses in Mark that show
him risen were apparently added later.)

The intractable complexities of fact produce the inevitable ambiguities
of faith. The more one knows, the less one knows. Was Jesus a carpenter, or
even a carpenter's son? The Greek word *tekton*, long taken to mean "carpenter," could mean something closer to a stoneworker or a day laborer. (One
thinks of the similar shadings of a word like "printer," which could refer
to Ben Franklin or to his dogsbody.) If a carpenter, then presumably he
was an artisan. If a stoneworker, then presumably he spent his early years
as a laborer, schlepping from Nazareth to the grand Greco-Roman city of
Sepphoris, nearby, to help build its walls and perhaps visit its theatre and
agora. And what of the term "Son of Man," which he uses again and again
in Mark, mysteriously: "The Son of Man is Lord even of the Sabbath." As
Diarmaid MacCulloch points out in his new, immensely ambitious and
absorbing history, *Christianity: The First Three Thousand Years*, the phrase,
which occurs in the Gospels "virtually exclusively in the reported words
of Jesus," certainly isn't at all the same as the later "Son of God," and may
merely be Aramaic for "folks like us."

Belief remains a bounce, faith a leap. Still, the appetite for historical
study of the New Testament remains a publishing constant and a popular
craze. Book after book—this year, ten in one month alone—appears, seeking the Truth. Paul Johnson has a sound believer's life, *Jesus: A Biography
from a Believer*, while Paul Verhoeven, the director of *Basic Instinct*, has
a new skeptical scholar's book, *Jesus of Nazareth*. Verhoeven turns out to
be a member of the Jesus Seminar, a collection mostly of scholars devoted
to reconstructing the historical Jesus, and much of what he has to say is
shrewd and learned. (An odd pull persists between box office and biblical
study. A few years ago, another big action film director and producer, James
Cameron, put himself at the center of a documentary called *The Lost Tomb
of Jesus*.[14])

14. Jacobovici, *Lost Tomb of Jesus*.

What the amateur reader wants, given the thickets of uncertainty that surround the garden, is not what the passionate polemicists want—not so much a verdict on whether Jesus was nasty or nice as a sense of what, if anything, was new in his preaching. Was the cult that changed the world a product of Paul's evangelism and imperial circumstance and the military embrace of one miracle-mystery cult among many such around? Or was there really something new, something unheard of, that can help explain the scale of what happened later? Did the rise of Christendom take place because historical plates were moving, with a poor martyred prophet caught between, or did one small pebble of parable and preaching start the avalanche that ended the antique world?

Ever since serious scholarly study of the Gospels began, in the nineteenth century, its moods have ranged from the frankly skeptical—including a "mythicist" position that the story is entirely made up—to the credulous, with some archeologists still holding that it is all pretty reliable, and tombs and traces can be found if you study the texts hard enough. The current scholarly tone is, judging from the new books, realist but pessimistic. While accepting a historical Jesus, the scholarship also tends to suggest that the search for him is a little like the search for the historical Sherlock Holmes: there were intellectual-minded detectives around, and Conan Doyle had one in mind in the eighteen-eighties, but the really interesting bits—Watson, Irene Adler, Moriarty, and the Reichenbach Falls—were, even if they all had remote real-life sources, shaped by the needs of storytelling, not by traces of truth. Holmes dies because heroes must, and returns from the dead, like Jesus, because the audience demanded it. (The view that the search for the historical Jesus is like the search for the historical Superman—that there's nothing there but a hopeful story and a girlfriend with an alliterative name—has by now been marginalized from the seminaries to the Internet; the scholar Earl Doherty defends it on his website with grace and tenacity.[15])

The American scholar Bart Ehrman has been explaining the scholars' truths for more than a decade now, in a series of sincere, quiet, and successful books. Ehrman is one of those best-selling authors like Richard Dawkins and Robert Ludlum and Peter Mayle, who write the same book over and over—but the basic template is so good that the new version is always worth reading. In his latest installment, *Jesus, Interrupted*, Ehrman once again shares with his readers the not entirely good news he found a

15. See https://www.jesuspuzzle.org.

quarter century ago when, after a fundamentalist youth, he went to graduate school: that all the Gospels were written decades after Jesus' death; that all were written in Greek, which Jesus and the apostles didn't speak and couldn't write (if they could read and write at all); and that they were written as testaments of faith, not chronicles of biography, shaped to fit a prophecy rather than report a profile.

The odd absences in Mark are matched by the unreal presences in the other Gospels. The beautiful nativity story in Luke, for instance, in which a Roman census forces the Holy Family to go back to its ancestral city of Bethlehem, is an obvious invention, since there was no empire-wide census at that moment, and no sane Roman bureaucrat would have dreamed of ordering people back to be counted in cities that their families had left hundreds of years before. The author of Luke, whoever he might have been, invented Bethlehem in order to put Jesus in David's city. (James Tabor, a professor of religious studies, in his 2006 book *The Jesus Dynasty*, takes surprisingly seriously the old Jewish idea that Jesus was known as the illegitimate son of a Roman soldier named Pantera—as well attested a tradition as any, occurring in Jewish texts of the second century, in which a Jesus ben Pantera makes several appearances, and the name is merely descriptive, not derogatory. Tabor has even found, however improbably, a tombstone in Germany for a Roman soldier from Syria-Palestine named Pantera.)

What seems a simple historical truth is that all the Gospels were written after the destruction of Jerusalem and the temple in the First Jewish-Roman War, in 70 CE—a catastrophe so large that it left the entire Jesus movement in a crisis that we can dimly imagine if we think of Jewish attitudes before and after the Holocaust: the scale of the tragedy leads us to see catastrophe as having been built into the circumstance. As L. Michael White's *Scripting Jesus: The Gospels in Rewrite* explains in daunting scholarly detail, even Mark—which, coming first, might seem to be closest to the truth—was probably written in the ruins of the temple and spiritually shaped to its desolate moment. Mark's essential point, he explains, is about secrecy: Jesus keeps telling people to be quiet about his miracles, and confides only to an inner circle of disciples.

With the temple gone, White says, it was necessary to persuade people that the grotesque political failure of Jesus' messianism wasn't a real failure. Mark invents the idea that Jesus' secret was not that he was the "Davidic" messiah, the Arthur-like returning king, but that he was someone even bigger: the Son of God, whose return would signify the end of time and the birth of the kingdom of God. The literary critic Frank Kermode, in *The Genesis of Secrecy* (1979), a pioneering attempt to read Mark seriously as poetic literature, made a similar point, though his is less historical than interpretative. Kermode considers Mark to be, as the French would say, a text that reads itself: the secret it contains is that its central figure is keeping a secret that we can never really get.

It is an intentionally open-ended story, prematurely closed, a mystery without a single solution.

Even if we make allowances for Mark's cryptic tracery, the human traits of his Jesus are evident: intelligence, short temper, and an ironic, dueling wit. What seems new about Jesus is not his piety or divine detachment but the humanity of his irritability and impatience. He's no Buddha. He gets annoyed at the stupidity of his followers, their inability to grasp an obvious point. "Do you have eyes but fail to see?" he asks the hapless disciples. The fine English actor Alec McCowen used to do a one-man show in which he recited Mark, complete, and his Jesus came alive instantly as a familiar human type—the Gandhi-Malcolm-Martin kind of charismatic leader of an oppressed people, with a character that clicks into focus as you begin to dramatize it. He's verbally spry and even a little shifty. He likes defiant, enigmatic paradoxes and pregnant parables that never quite close, perhaps by design. A story about a vineyard whose ungrateful husbandmen keep killing the servants sent to them is an antiestablishment, even an anticlerical story, but it isn't so obvious as to get him in trouble. The suspicious priests keep trying to catch him out in a declaration of anti-Roman sentiment: Is it lawful to give tribute to Caesar or not, they ask—that is, do you recognize Roman authority or don't you? He has a penny brought out, sees the picture of the emperor on it, and, shrugging, says to give to the state everything that rightly belongs to the state. The brilliance of that famous crack is that Jesus turns the question back on the questioner, in mock innocence. Why, you give the king the king's things and God God's. Of course, this leaves open the real question: What is Caesar's and what is God's? It's a tautology designed to evade self-incrimination.

Jesus' morality has a brash, sidewise indifference to conventional ideas of goodness. His pet style blends the epigrammatic with the enigmatic. When he makes that complaint about the prophet having no honor in his own hometown, or says exasperatedly that there is no point in lighting a candle unless you intend to put it in a candlestick, his voice carries a disdain for the props of piety that still feels startling. And so with the tale of the boy who wastes his inheritance but gets a feast from his father, while his dutiful brother doesn't; or the one about the weeping whore who is worthier than her good, prim onlookers; or about the passionate Mary who is better than her hardworking sister Martha. There is a wild gaiety about Jesus' moral teachings that still leaps off the page. He is informal in a new way, too, that remains unusual among prophets. MacCulloch points out that he continually addresses God as "Abba," Father, or even Dad, and that the expression translated in the King James Version as a solemn "Verily I say unto you" is actually a quirky Aramaic throat clearer, like Dr. Johnson's "Depend upon it, Sir."

Some of the sayings do have, in their contempt for material prosperity, the ring of Greek Cynic philosophy, but there is also something neither quite Greek nor quite Jewish about Jesus' morality that makes it fresh and strange even now. Is there a more miraculous scene in ancient literature than the one in John where Jesus absentmindedly writes on the ground while his fellow Jews try to entrap him into approving the stoning of an adulteress, only to ask, wide eyed, if it wouldn't be a good idea for the honor of throwing the first stone to be given to the man in the mob who hasn't sinned himself? Is there a more compressed and charming religious exhortation than the one in the Gospel of Thomas in which Jesus merrily recommends to his disciples, "Be passersby"? Too much fussing about place and home and ritual, and even about where, exactly, you're going to live, is unnecessary: be wanderers, dharma bums.

This social radicalism still shines through—not a programmatic radicalism of national revolution but one of Kerouac-like satori-seeking-on-the-road. And the social radicalism is highly social. The sharpest opposition in the Gospels, the scholar and former priest John Dominic Crossan points out in his illuminating books—*The Historical Jesus: The Life of a Mediterranean Jewish Peasant* is the best known—is between John the Faster and Jesus the Feaster. Jesus eats and drinks with whores and highwaymen, turns water into wine, and, finally, in one way or another, establishes a mystical union at a feast through its humble instruments of bread and wine.

The table is his altar in every sense. Crossan, the cofounder of the Jesus Seminar, makes a persuasive case that Jesus' fressing was perhaps the most radical element in his life—that his table manners pointed the way to his heavenly morals. Crossan sees Jesus living within a Mediterranean Jewish peasant culture, a culture of clan and cohort, in which who eats with whom defines who stands where and why. So the way Jesus repeatedly violates the rules on eating, on "commensality," would have shocked his contemporaries. He dines with people of a different social rank, which would have shocked most Romans, and with people of different tribal allegiance, which would have shocked most Jews. The most forceful of his sayings, still shocking to any pious Jew or Muslim, is "What goes into a man's mouth does not make him unclean, but what comes out of his mouth, that is what makes him unclean." Jesus isn't a hedonist or an epicurean, but he clearly isn't an ascetic, either: he feeds the multitudes rather than instructing them how to go without. He's interested in saving people living normal lives, buying and selling what they can, rather than in retreating into the company of those who have already arrived at a moral conclusion about themselves.

To a modern reader, the relaxed egalitarianism of the open road and the open table can seem undermined by the other part of Jesus' message, a violent and even vengeful prediction of a final judgment and a large-scale damnation. In Mark, Jesus is both a fierce apocalyptic prophet who is preaching the death of the world—he says categorically that the end is near—and a wise philosophical teacher who professes love for his neighbor and supplies advice for living. If the end is near, why give so much sage counsel? If human life is nearly over, why preach in such detail the right way to live? One argument is that a later, perhaps "unpersonified" body of hellenized wisdom literature was tacked on to an earlier account of a Jewish messianic prophet. Since both kinds of literature—apocalyptic hysterics and stoic sayings—can be found all over the period, perhaps they were merely wrenched together.

And yet a single figure who "projects" two personae at the same time, or in close sequence, one dark and one dreamy, is a commonplace among charismatic prophets. That's what a charismatic prophet is: someone whose aura of personal conviction manages to reconcile a hard doctrine with a humane manner. The leaders of the African American community before the civil rights era, for instance, had to be both prophets and political agitators to an oppressed and persecuted people in a way not unlike that of the real Jesus (and all the other forgotten zealots and rabbis whom the first-century Jewish historian Josephus names and sighs over). They, too, tended to oscillate between the comforting and the catastrophic. Malcolm X was the very model of a modern apocalyptic prophet-politician, unambiguously preaching violence and a doctrine of millennial revenge, all fueled by a set of cult beliefs—a hovering UFO, a strange racial myth. But Malcolm was also a community builder, a moral reformer (genuinely distraught over the sexual sins of his leader), who refused to carry weapons, and who ended, within the constraints of his faith, as some kind of universalist. When he was martyred, he was called a prophet of hate; within three decades of his death—about the time that separates the Gospels from Jesus—he could be the cover subject of a liberal humanist magazine like this one. One can even see how martyrdom and "beatification" draws out more personal detail, almost perfectly on schedule: Alex Haley, Malcolm's Paul, is long on doctrine and short on details; thirty years on, Spike Lee, his Mark, has a full role for a wife and children, and a universalist message that manages to blend Malcolm into Mandela. (As if to prove this point, just the other week came news of suppressed chapters of Haley's *Autobiography*, which, according to Malcolm's daughter, "showed too much of my father's humanity.")

As the Bacchae knew, we always tear our Gods to bits, and eat the bits we like. Still, a real, unchangeable difference does exist between what might be called storytelling truths and statement-making truths—between what makes credible, if sweeping, sense in a story and what's required for a close-knit metaphysical argument. Certain kinds of truths are convincing only in a narrative. The idea, for instance, that the ring of power should be given to two undersized amateurs to throw into a volcano at the very center of the enemy's camp makes sound and sober sense, of a kind, in Tolkien; but you would never expect to find it as a premise at the Middle Earth Military Academy. Anyone watching Hamlet will find his behavior completely understandable—OK, I buy it; he's toying with his uncle—though any critic thinking about it afterward will reflect that this behavior is a little nuts.

In Mark, Jesus' divinity unfolds without quite making sense intellectually, and without ever needing to. It has the hypnotic flow of dramatic movement. The story is one of self-discovery: he doesn't know who he is and then he begins to think he does and then he doubts and in pain and glory he dies and is known. The story works. But, as a proposition under scrutiny, it makes intolerable demands on logic. If Jesus is truly one with God, in what sense could he suffer doubt, fear, exasperation, pain, horror, and so on? So we get the Jesus rendered in the book of John, who doesn't. But if he doesn't suffer doubt, fear, exasperation, pain, and horror, in what sense is his death a sacrifice rather than just a theatrical enactment? A lamb whose throat is not cut and does not bleed is not really much of an offering.

None of this is very troubling if one has a pagan idea of divinity: the Son of God might then be half human and half divine, suffering and triumphing and working out his heroic destiny in the half-mortal way of

Hercules, for instance. But that's ruled out by the full weight of the Jewish idea of divinity—omnipresent and omniscient, knowing all and seeing all. If God he was—not some Hindu-ish avatar or offspring of God, but actually one with God—then God once was born and had dirty diapers and took naps. The longer you think about it, the more astounding, or absurd, it becomes. To be really believed at all, it can only be told again.

So the long history of the early church councils that tried to make the tales into a theology is, in a way, a history of coming out of the movie confused, and turning to someone else to ask what just happened. This is the subject of Philip Jenkins's *Jesus Wars: How Four Patriarchs, Three Queens, and Two Emperors Decided What Christians Would Believe for the Next 1,500 Years.* Jenkins explains what was at stake in the seemingly wacky wars over the Arian heresy—the question of whether Jesus the Son shared an essence with God the Father or merely a substance—which consumed the Western world through the second and third centuries. Was Jesus one with God in the sense that, say, Sean Connery is one with Daniel Craig, different faces of a single role, or in the sense that James Bond is one with Ian Fleming, each so dependent on the other that one cannot talk about the creation apart from its author? The passion with which people argued over apparently trivial word choices was, Jenkins explains, not a sign that they were specially sensitive to theology. People argued that way because they were part of social institutions—cities, schools, clans, networks—in which words are banners and pennants: who pledged to whom was inseparable from who said what in what words. It wasn't that they really cared about the conceptual difference between the claim that Jesus and the Father were *homoousian* (same in essence) and the claim that the two were *homoiousian* (same in substance); they cared about whether the Homoousians or the Homoiousians were going to run the church.

The effort to seal off the inspiration from the intolerance, nice Jesus from nasty Jesus, is very old. Jefferson compiled his own New Testament, with the ethical teachings left in and the miracles and damnations left out—and that familiar, outraged sense of the ugly duplicity of the Christian heritage is at the heart of Philip Pullman's new plaint against it, *The Good Man Jesus and the Scoundrel Christ,* in which the two aspects are neatly divided into twins borne by Mary. The wise Jesus is brother to the shrewd Christ. One leads to the nice Jewish boy, the other to Paul's scary punitive God. Pullman, a writer of great skill and feeling, as he has shown in his magical children's fantasies, feels the betrayal of Jesus by his brother Christ as a fundamental betrayal of humanity. He wants us to forget Christ and return to Jesus alone, to surrender miracles for morals. Pullman's book, however, is not narrowly polemical; he also retells the parables and acts with a lucid simplicity that strips away the Pauline barnacles. His real achievement is to translate Jesus' sayings into a simple, almost childlike English that would seem to have much of the sound we are told is present in the artless original Greek: "Those who make peace between enemies, those who solve bitter disputes—they will be blessed. But beware, and remember what I tell you: there are some who will be cursed, who will never inherit the Kingdom of God. D'you want to know who they are? Here goes: Those who are rich will be cursed."

If one thing seems clear from all the scholarship, though, it's that Paul's divine Christ came first, and Jesus the wise rabbi came later. This fixed, steady twoness at the heart of the Christian story can't be wished away by liberal hope any more than it could be resolved by theological hair-splitting. Its intractability is part of the intoxication of belief. It can be amputated, mystically married, revealed as a fraud, or worshipped as the greatest of mysteries. The two go on, and their twoness is what distinguishes the faith and gives it its discursive dynamism. All faiths have fights, but, as MacCulloch shows at intricate, thousand-page length, few have so many super-subtle shadings of dogma: wine or blood, flesh or wafer, one God in three spirits or three Gods in one; a song of children, stables, psalms, parables, and peacemakers, on the one hand, a threnody of suffering, nails, wild dogs, and damnation and risen God, on the other. The two spin around each other throughout history—the remote Pantocrator of Byzantium giving way to the suffering man of the Renaissance, and on and on.

It is typical of this conundrum that, in the past century, the best Christian poet, W. H. Auden, and the greatest anti-Christian polemicist, William Empson, were exact contemporaries, close friends, and, as slovenly social types, almost perfectly interchangeable Englishmen. Auden chose Christianity for the absolute democracy of its vision—there is, in it, "neither Jew nor German, East nor West, boy nor girl, smart nor dumb, boss nor worker." Empson, in the same period, beginning in the fatal nineteen-forties, became the most articulate critic of a morality reduced "to keeping the taboos imposed by an infinite malignity," in which the reintroduction of human sacrifice as a sacred principle left the believer with "no sense either of personal honor or of the public good." (In this case, though, where Auden saw a nice Christ, Empson saw a nasty Jesus.)

Beyond the words, we still hear that cry. The passion is still the point. In Mark, Jesus' arrest and execution feels persuasively less preordained and willed than accidental and horrific. Jesus seems to have an intimation of the circumstance he has found himself in—leading a rebellion against Rome that is not really a rebellion, yet doesn't really leave any possibility of retreat—and some corner of his soul wants no part of it: "Abba, Father, everything is possible for you. Take away this cup from me." Mel Gibson was roughed up for roughing up Jesus, in his *Passion of the Christ*, but, though Gibson can fairly be accused of fanaticism, he can't be accused of unfairness: in the long history of human cruelty, crucifixion, practiced as a mass punishment by the Romans, was uniquely horrible. The victim was stripped, in order to be deprived of dignity, then paraded, then whipped bloody, and then left to die as slowly as possible in as public a manner as conceivable. (In a sign of just how brutal it was, Josephus tells us that he begged the Roman rulers for three of his friends to be taken off the cross after they had spent hours on it; one lived.) The victim's legs were broken to bring death in a blaze of pain. And the corpse was generally left to be eaten by wild dogs. It was terrifying and ever present.

Verhoeven, citing Crossan, offers an opening scene for a Jesus biopic which neatly underlines this point. He imagines a man being nailed to a cross, cries of agony, two companion crosses in view, and then we crane out to see two hundred crosses and two hundred victims: we are at the beginning of the story, the mass execution of Jewish rebels in 4 BC, not the end. This was the Roman death waiting for rebels from the outset, and Jesus knew it. Jesus' cry of desolation—"My God, my God, why have you forsaken me?"—though primly edited out or explained as an apropos quotation from the Psalms by later evangelists, pierces us even now from the pages of Mark, across all the centuries and Church comforts. The shock and pity of failure still resonates.

One thing, at least, the cry assures: the Jesus faith begins with a failure of faith. His Father let him down, and the promise wasn't kept. "Some who are standing here will not taste death before they see the kingdom of God," Jesus announced; but none of them did. Jesus, and Paul following him, says unambiguously that whatever is coming is coming soon—that the end is very, very near. It wasn't, and the whole of what follows is built on an apology for what went wrong. The seemingly modern waiver, "Well, I know he said that, but he didn't really mean it quite the way it sounded," is built right into the foundation of the cult. The sublime symbolic turn—or the retreat to metaphor, if you prefer—begins with the first words of the faith. If the kingdom of God proved elusive, he must have meant that the kingdom of God was inside, or outside, or above, or yet to come, anything other than what the words seem so plainly to have meant.

The argument is the reality, and the absence of certainty the certainty. Authority and fear can circumscribe the argument, or congeal it, but can't end it. In the beginning was the word: in the beginning, and in the middle, and right there at the close, Word without end, Amen. The impulse of orthodoxy has always been to suppress the wrangling as a sign of weakness; the impulse of more modern theology is to embrace it as a sign of life. The deeper question is whether the uncertainty at the center mimics the plurality of possibilities essential to liberal debate, as the more open-minded theologians like to believe, or is an antique mystery in a story open only as the tomb is open, with a mystery left inside, never to be entirely explored or explained. With so many words over so long a time, perhaps passersby can still hear tones inaudible to the more passionate participants.

Somebody seems to have hoped so, once.

7

What Does the Crucifixion Signify?

JACK MILES IS A polymath—in religion, literature, Near Eastern languages, and life. He has won the Pulitzer Prize and the MacArthur Foundation's "Genius Grant," among others. He was the general editor of the monumental two-volume, four-thousand-page *Norton Anthology of World Religions* (2014).

Miles brings to the study of religion interpretive gifts honed through years of experience as an editor and critic. His book *God: A Biography* studies how the character of God changes during the Old Testament. His sequel *Christ: A Crisis in the Life of God* shows how Jesus was the answer to God's own failures in fulfilling his promises to the chosen people of Israel. The New Testament universalized God's people: the good news of Jesus Christ is extended to everyone in the world, Jew and gentile alike. Christ also signified what Miles calls "the self-disarmament of God," in the sense that God no longer would wage earthly wars.

DISCUSSION QUESTIONS

"War, Peace, and a Crisis in the Life of God"

1. Bach's *St. Matthew Passion* (1727) is considered by some people to be the greatest masterpiece of Western sacred music. It depicts the final days of the life of Jesus.

While in his forties, Jack Miles heard it as if for the first time. He was transformed. "What struck me with an emotional power that I had never felt before, an emotional power that rose exegetically, as it were, from the music, was that this Lamb of God, this slain and sacrificed lamb, was God himself."

Miles *knew* this idea well from his decade becoming a Jesuit. But now, "in the poem set to Bach's magnificent music," Miles suddenly *felt* it.[1]

Listen yourself to the beginning of Bach's *St. Matthew Passion* (less than seven minutes).[2] And if you would like to read St. Matthew's passion in Matthew 26–27, see below for a link.[3]

Now think of your own life. When has a work of art suddenly enabled you to *feel* something you already *knew* well?

"Crucifixion and the Conscience of the West"

1. Friedrich Nietzsche "had seen, and seen correctly, something utterly shocking at the heart of the Christian myth, a 'frightening hidden premise' to which the genteel Christianity of the late nineteenth century had grown numb": the divinization of the victim.[4]

   a. What does this "premise" mean? Why did it shock Nietzsche?

   b. Why do you think "genteel Christianity" would want to be numbed to the divinization of the victim?

2. The first convert to Christianity outside Palestine was a black eunuch who was converted by reading this passage:

   He was oppressed and afflicted, yet he did not open his mouth; he was led like a lamb to the slaughter, and as a sheep before its shearers is silent, so he did not open his mouth. By oppression and judgment he was taken away. Yet who of his generation protested?

1. Miles, "War, Peace, and Crisis," this vol., 113.

2. For example, at https://www.youtube.com/watch?v=j4Efeafzv9c.

3. https://www.biblegateway.com/passage/?search=Matthew%2026–27&version =NIV.

4. Miles, "Crucifixion and Conscience," this vol., 120.

For he was cut off from the land of the living; for the transgression of my people he was punished. (Isa 53:7–8 NIV)

    a. Why do you think this passage had such a radical, perspective-shifting effect on this man?

    b. How does the passage resonate with you?

3. The final paragraph of "Crucifixion and the Conscience of the West" begins, "The world is a great crime, and someone must be made to pay for it."[5] How would you interpret both parts of that sentence?

    a. What is that "great crime"?

    b. And if "someone" can be "made to pay for it"—so what? Why would that matter?

5. Miles, "Crucifixion and Conscience," this vol., 126.

War, Peace, and a Crisis in the Life of God

JACK MILES

My story begins with two memories of war. Neither memory is mine except indirectly. Both are stories that my mother has told me about my very young self. I was born seven months after Pearl Harbor. My father, as an employee of the Commonwealth Edison Company in Chicago, deemed at the time a strategic industry, and as the father of a newborn, was not immediately drafted. However, as casualties rose, the fateful call finally came. When it did, I was just past my second birthday. My little sister, Mary Anne, who had arrived in the interim, was seven months old. For weeks after my father left for Camp Crowder in Missouri (the name Camp Crowder is one of my earliest verbal memories), it seems that I refused to eat dinner. I would explain, my mother tells me, that we didn't eat dinner until Daddy came home from work. Night after night, I refused to believe that he wouldn't come home if we just waited a little longer. Because her own deepest fear was that one night or other she might learn that her husband truly would never come home, hearing these words coming from my mouth was almost more than she could bear at times. That's the first memory.

The second memory—again, not mine but hers—is of my reading a few years later in the *Chicago Daily News* an early, grisly account of the Bataan Death March—a brutal forced march in the Philippines of American soldiers captured by the Japanese. I could decode the words, but at age six I could scarcely begin to cope with the content, and I burst into tears. Among other immaturities of understanding, I could not believe that Japanese soldiers would not show up at our front door to take my father away and do to him what they had done to their American captives in the Philippines. In a quite similar way, I could not grasp that Roman soldiers like those who under King Herod had slaughtered all male infants under the age of two in the Gospel according to Matthew, would not show up at our front door and demand my baby brother, Terry. I was precocious, you might well say, and yet not quite precocious enough.

Physical violence—war, in a word—has played a key role in the genesis of what even enthusiastic reviewers of *God: A Biography* have called my peculiar approach to the Bible. To the extent that an author can ever know such a thing about his own work, I find the distant origin of that book and its sequel *Christ: A Crisis in the Life of God* in the nightmares of a little boy who began worrying about war as soon as he could talk.

I turned seven in midsummer 1949. Mine was a Roman Catholic family, and in the months before Easter all second-graders in my parochial school took instruction for our First Holy Communion. As this instruction was being imparted, in February 1950, Sen. Joseph McCarthy terrified America by announcing that he had in his possession a long list of Communist agents secretly working at high levels in our federal government. Many Americans received this report as today we might receive a report that agents of Osama Bin Laden had penetrated the Federal Aviation Administration.

McCarthy's innuendos triggered a chain reaction of ever more frightening rumors. Things got so out of hand that the nun who was preparing my class for our First Holy Communion told us sorrowfully that Joseph Stalin and Harry Truman had secretly met in the White House itself. This hair-raising report sailed right over my classmates' heads. Unfortunately for me, I had been reading about the Russians in the newspaper; and learning that they were about to take over the presidency, I once again burst into tears and had to be escorted to the office of Sister Mary Demetria, the Sister Superior.

Sister Mary Demetria, I am happy to say, was no paranoid but a woman of deep and humane wisdom. My conversation with her that day, early as it came in my life, stands as a kind of turning point. It was then that I learned the paradox that a large sorrow can sometimes soothe the pain of a small one. Of the alleged Truman-Stalin conspiracy, she said only that this rumor was unconfirmed. She added, though, that she was sure many of the rumors flying around would prove false. "Don't believe everything you hear," she told a seven-year-old who, by and large, did believe everything he heard: another simple but crucial lesson in how to maintain one's political composure.

As for the Cold War, however, to her great credit, she did not try to hide it from me, young as I was. Instead, she did what she could to show me that even the superpower standoff, terrifying as it was, could become less terrifying when you understood its context. Her way of providing context was not immediately religious, but it became religious before she was finished. She began in the classic manner of all wisdom literature by sinking my individual sorrow, my individual fear, in the general human condition. She had a large rotating globe in her office, and she stood me next to it while she turned it slowly and pointed to one place after another where war was raging at that very moment: Jews against Arabs, Indians against Pakistanis, Greeks against Turks, a civil war that had left millions starving in China, and so forth. All this bad news ought to have further upset me, but it did not. It made my sorrow, and even the true danger to my country, seem smaller against the panorama of all the other violence in the world. Before sending me back to class, we knelt down and said a prayer in her office for world peace.

Sister Mary Demetria's therapy worked so well for me that several months later, in June 1950, when President Truman declared war on North Korea, my best buddy and I rode around the neighborhood on our Communion bicycles cheerfully crowing, "Truman declares war! Truman declares war!" Deep down, though, I was a little less cheerful than my pal. Through the rest of that year, I followed the progress of the war in the newspapers with a degree of attention beyond my years. Toward the end of 1950, or just after I entered third grade, President Truman—a man more mocked than admired in our neighborhood—sacked the legendary Gen. Douglas MacArthur for incompetence and insubordination in commanding the American troops in Korea. You would have thought, however, and I did think, from the tumultuous reception MacArthur received on his return home, that it was the president rather than the general who owed the nation an apology. In New York, a ticker tape parade up Broadway was followed, after dark, by a melodramatic, floodlit rally at the Polo Grounds. When MacArthur said, "Old soldiers don't die, they just fade away," millions of eyes overflowed with tears, millions of hearts burned with righteous anger. A mighty throng sang "God Bless America," and talk began to spread that MacArthur should run for president. A few even said he should become president without waiting for an election.

Thank God, it didn't happen that way. A better soldier, Dwight Eisenhower, stood for election in the ordinary way and became a better president than MacArthur would ever have made. As for me, sometime in 1951, I disappeared into a reasonable facsimile of the happy anesthesia of American childhood. I acquired, in other words, an almost if not quite normal sense of security and immunity that lasted for the next ten years, or until I turned eighteen and had to register for the draft.

Mine was a lower-middle-class social stratum in which no one of my parents' generation went to college and no one, male or female, ever thought of career. The word *career* was used, oddly enough, only of women, and then only, with a certain sadness, in the phrase *career woman*. A career woman was a woman who had never married and had no family to fill her life with pride and joy. A career woman had a wardrobe better than Mom's and wore more jewelry and makeup than she did, but a career woman had to go to work every day; and when she came home, it was to the silence of an apartment full of precious, breakable things that no one with kids would dream of owning or ever really want in the first place.

As for the career man, the species simply did not exist. Men did not have careers. Men had jobs, and men were never happier than when they could leave the job and come home to the family.

For the news-hungry reader that I had continued to be, however, one other idea did creep in at the margins, a career idea and not a job idea, and that was the idea of newspaper reporting. Each day, my father left early in the morning to take the bus and the elevated train to work. Each afternoon, he came walking back home with his lunch bucket in one hand and, in the other, the *Chicago Daily News* that he had read during the ride home. Picking up the *Daily News* wherever he dropped it and reading it spread out on the living room carpet, I gradually hatched the notion that though nobody like these reporters lived on a street like ours, most of them did seem to live somewhere in the Great City of Chicago. Their work seemed to me something I could almost imagine doing myself, though for some reason this was a secret I shared with nobody.

As it happened, there existed at that time—there may still exist, for all I know—an organization called the Serra Club whose members, enlightened and rather well-to-do Catholic laymen, were on the lookout for able but underprivileged Catholic boys who did *not* want to become priests but might well be the future lay leadership of the church. When I was a high school senior, and editor of the school newspaper, this group awarded me a fabulous blank-check college scholarship. All reasonable expenses would be paid, whatever they were. Moreover, quietly declaring their independence from the clergy, they informed me that I could take my scholarship to any college, Catholic or not, that would accept me.

The school I wanted to attend was Northwestern University, in Evanston, Illinois, home of the Medill School of Journalism, where I had attended a summer program for high school students after my junior year. Northwestern met with the approval of the Serra Club, but then two things happened, two things that were connected, though I didn't see the connection at the time, two moments heavy with echoes from the traumatic early experiences with which I began.

First, in the company of my father, whose presence had made the moment seem all the graver, I registered for the draft. I did not guess—no one did in 1960—that over the next fifteen years, fifty thousand American lives would be sacrificed to the vanity of leaders who could not admit that they had made a terrible strategic mistake in a fully legitimate struggle against Communism. And yet there was already something ominous in the air. John Kennedy and Richard Nixon were both making American vulnerability the rhetorical center of their presidential campaigns. Kennedy claimed, falsely, that Eisenhower and Nixon had let a "missile gap" open up between the Russians and us. Nixon hinted, with no more evidence than Kennedy had of his missile gap, that Kennedy was a reckless liberal who would lead America into military peril. What mattered was that both men presented the United States as engaged in an apocalyptic struggle of ultimate good against ultimate evil. The Sancho Panzas of the world, wiser than the Don Quixotes, take this sort of thing with a grain of salt. The Don Quixotes, and I am a Don Quixote, find such rhetoric at once terrifying and intoxicating.

Connected, psychologically, to the experience of registering for the draft while the two presidential candidates competed with one another in alarming the American public was something that happened during my senior class religious retreat. A charismatic Jesuit preacher evoked for us boys a scene drawn from the Spiritual Exercises of St. Ignatius Loyola, the founder of the Jesuits. He told us with somber eloquence to imagine a vast plain, and on it two immense armies, each stretching as far as the eye could see. One army was captained by Christ the King, the other by Satan. In our mind's eye, we were to see Christ—noble, self-sacrificing, asking everything of his followers, but asking nothing of them that he has not already given himself. And then we were to see Satan—cruel, tyrannical, egotistical, taking everything from his followers, and giving nothing but fatal illusion in return. Despite the fact that the devil had long since become a metaphor for me, I found it easy to surrender myself to this hour-long exercise in guided imagery, for I was living in a country that believed that good and evil were engaged in a cosmic struggle. Long before President Ronald Reagan used the phrase, millions of Americans believed that the Soviet Union was an Evil Empire. But were we a Holy Empire? No one really believed that; and as a boy of eighteen, I was honestly searching for that great good with which I might wholeheartedly ally myself. Where, if anywhere, could it be found?

The retreat master had given our retreat a kind of theme song or leit-motif in the Latin phrase *Quid hoc ad aeternitatem?* (What is this to eternity?). I had and still have a fatal weakness for noble sentiments expressed in foreign languages. Before the retreat was over, I had made my decision: the Society of Jesus, the Jesuit order itself, would be my great cause, my existential solution.

And so I handed back my blank-check scholarship and gave up journalism, forever as I thought. What did the Jesuits have? Well, the motto of the French Foreign Legion is—another of those thrilling Latin phrases—*Legio patria mea* (The legion is my fatherland)—the legion, note well, not France. I was far less committed to Roman Catholicism as a form of Christianity than I was in love with the romance of the Society of Jesus as something like the foreign legion of the Catholic Church, proudly intellectual and yet arrayed like an army on the battlefield of history. Conveniently, I blush to recall, my enlistment in this exalted army meant that I would never be drafted by that other army. All Jesuits, as members of a religious order, enjoy the clerical exemption from military service.

I spent the 1960s almost to the day as a Jesuit, leaving the order, without rancor, when I could no longer deny that the Church, finally, did have to come before the Society of Jesus just as France, finally, did have to come before the French Foreign Legion. And as the Catholic claim on truth became a more pressing theoretical question, celibacy became suddenly a much more pressing practical question. I left the order in 1970, lost my virginity in a big hurry, then drifted away from the church itself and for several years had no institutional relationship with Christianity in any form. About ten years after leaving the Jesuits, while living with the woman who would become my wife, I found my way back to Christianity through the welcoming portals of the Episcopal Church. As for my work life, though I had completed a PhD in Hebrew Bible at Harvard University, I found my way in short order out of academe into book publishing and on into the journalism that had been my first love and my first goal.

I had become a Bible scholar, you see, largely because while still operating as a loyal Jesuit in Christ's foreign legion, I was asked to do so. Acquiring a doctorate in Old Testament was not, in the first place, my idea, but I knew as well as my superiors did that I was good at learning foreign languages, and I knew that this was if not truly the key skill, then at least for most the main obstacle. When my superiors asked if I would take on this challenge, I saluted smartly, in effect, and marched off to Harvard. There was, of course, the minor detail of winning acceptance at the Harvard Graduate School of Arts and Sciences, but the Department of Near Eastern Languages and Literatures, where the study of the Hebrew Bible was housed, had had a more or less happy experience with Jesuits who had preceded me, and they let me in.

We are now up to the academic year 1966–1967, the year of the Six-Day War in Israel. I spent this year as a special student at the Hebrew University in Jerusalem, preparing for Harvard by studying Hebrew and archaeology. In the following academic year, 1967–1968, I was at Harvard, and the spring of 1968 proved to be the wildest single season in a decade of unrest. Every Sunday, the Cambridge Common was blue with marijuana smoke, and rage against the war in Vietnam was at fever pitch.

Two years or so later, though I was near the end of my doctorate, I considered calling the whole thing off as not my idea in the first place. My private romance with the Jesuits was rapidly coming to an end, and with it whatever vague hope I had entertained that the Bible could be made to function as a revolutionary manifesto for the Catholic Church. I began to think of the Church as somehow somebody else's responsibility, not mine. As for the Bible as an academic subject, I was unexcited by Harvard's approach to it because I was unexcited by history as a discipline. Essential as history is to the adult mind, I have always seen it not as the drama but merely as stage upon which the drama is performed. Bible scholarship that sought to write the history of Israel followed by the life of Jesus and then by the history of the early church—all this as a grand epic for which the Bible was merely one source among others—came seem somebody else's life work, not mine. What had always privately excited me—the game I loved, the sport in which I refused to surrender my amateur status—was imaginative literature, and this was a game that by and large established Bible scholarship did not play with any enthusiasm.

During the years after my graduation from Harvard, my contacts in private life with unbelievers and with unaffiliated questioners who did not care to be pinned down even by so flexible a label as *agnostic* grew ever wider. As they did, I became ever more persuaded that these people were more like me than they were like my teachers. The historicity of the Bible— the sorting out of what had happened from what had not, what had really been said from what had not—did not much excite them. When they read the Bible at all, they read it rather as they would read the *Iliad*. In such a reading, God was important in the one classic as and only as Zeus was important in the other. In either case, the relevant importance was *to the story.*

Thinking of these people and of myself as someone who might have something to say to them, I ventured a brief but programmatic essay in 1972 entitled "The Debut of the Bible as a Pagan Classic." I was new enough to publishing, and naïve enough in general, to be crestfallen when the response to it was utter silence. I had hoped to find at least somebody to talk to or correspond with. In retrospect, I could perhaps have looked a little harder, but I did not. There was, as ever, a job shortage for humanities PhDs. Unsure whether I really had anything to say, doubtful that anyone much wanted to hear it, I began to think that I should quit the field after all. Three years later, when I finally did so, what I felt was a profound relief. It was a pleasure, after working for so long a time in or near religious institutions, to say goodbye to them and feel myself free to be completely secular if this were my choice. I did miss the flexible schedule and summer holidays of academic life for a year or two, but then all that slipped into my past as well. From a transitional position as religion editor at Doubleday in New York, I moved with pleasure to one as philosophy editor at the University of California Press in Los Angeles, then to one as literary editor at the *Los Angeles Times*, and finally to a seat on that newspaper's editorial board, where I wrote increasingly on foreign affairs, most especially on the war in Bosnia. For professional and even for most personal purposes, I was done with the Bible.

And then something befell me that quite unexpectedly returned the Bible to me or me to the Bible. Sometime in the mid- to late 1980s, I heard—perhaps for the first time, perhaps only with full attention for the first time—J. S. Bach's *St. Matthew Passion*. In the opening measures of the antiphonal chorus that begins that masterpiece, a crowd of Jesus' disciples grieves over the suffering inflicted on him. They sing back and forth to one another:

> See him!
> Whom?

The bridegroom!
See him!
How?
As if a lamb.

Now the fact that Jesus had suffered was obviously nothing new to me. It is nothing new to anyone in the Western world. Equally familiar was the pathos of referring to Jesus as the Lamb of God. What struck me with an emotional power that I had never felt before, an emotional power that rose exegetically, as it were, from the music, was that this Lamb of God, this slain and sacrificed lamb, was God himself.

God himself turned into a sacrificial animal by his own decision! The pathos in the juxtaposition of the image of the bridegroom—the male of the human species at his peak of beauty, sexuality, and joy—with the image of the slaughtered beast was in itself almost too horrifying to bear. But this was just the beginning: In both the Old Testament and the New, the word *bridegroom* typically refers to the bridegroom *of Israel*—that is, to God himself. Again and again, God uses the marriage metaphor to characterize his relationship with his chosen people. So, in the poem set to Bach's magnificent music, the slain lamb was also the slain *divine* bridegroom.

But immediately there arose a staggering contradiction. God, the bridegroom of Israel, was also God, the champion of Israel, the fierce and invincible warrior who drowned the army of Pharaoh in the Red Sea. Among the various images that his people had employed to characterize him, he was their rock, their lion, their sword, and their shield. Well, then: What had befallen this warrior that, having taken on human form, he had fallen so inconceivably out of character? Extreme reversals of behavior typically betray extreme pressures of one sort or another. What extreme pressure had been brought to bear upon God that he had undergone so unthinkable a transformation, losing what had for centuries seemed the very core of his identity?

My answer to this question took years to formulate and entailed reconceiving the plot of the Bible—the only available explanation for this change of character—in a new and somewhat disturbing way. What sort of research was relevant for this kind of reflection? Anything might help, and yet much might hinder. My strong suspicion was that everything I needed was in plain view, easily within reach, and yet not noticed in the way it needed to be noticed. I was like a man who has mislaid something on his desk and has no alternative but to spend a good deal of time staring at the desktop—in my case, just reading the Bible—until he sees it. Outside opinions are likely to be of limited utility.

What I had, in short, after my *St. Matthew Passion* experience was more an obscure but powerful motive than a clear program. The power of this motive, and perhaps its obscurity as well, stemmed from the fact that it provided me a way to speak through the Bible about my own lifelong obsession with warfare as a threat to those I love and to myself. The inchoate program connected with it provided a way for me to exploit the biblical metaphor that had been most effectively and even brilliantly taught during my years at Harvard—namely, the identity-structuring metaphor of divine warfare. My way of using this metaphor would yield literary rather than historical criticism. But how could all this be brought about?

Eventually, I decided on a kind of interpretive experiment. For the purposes of this experiment, I would postulate that God's Incarnation as a Jew who, like a lamb, would not resist his own execution was the resolution of a prior conflict, a prior crisis in his own life. And because this striking change so affected God's identity as a warrior, I further postulated that a war of some kind must have provoked the change. In the end, I defined the crisis in God's life as his failure to keep his word to Israel that after the nation's terrible defeat by Babylonia, he would restore it to sovereignty and glory. God never did keep that promise. At the time when he was born and died as the Jew Jesus, five hundred years had gone by, and still the promise was unkept. Moreover, God knew that Rome, the new Babylon, was about to wreak worse destruction upon his people than Babylonia had ever attempted, worse than any empire would again attempt until the Third Reich. God knew that this holocaust, this shoah, was coming, and he knew that he would do nothing to stop it. This was the crisis in his life that made him become not merely a Jew but a Jew who would be crucified as the whole Jewish nation would be crucified in Rome's ghastly Jewish Wars. Nothing less violent than that would suffice to demonstrate a revision in the very identity of God.

And yet God had another problem, deeper and older and more painful even than this one. In a fit of violent anger, he had disfigured near the very start the beauty of his own creation. On the sixth day, he had said, famously, "It is good." But not long after that, when his human creatures succumbed to temptation by the serpent that God himself, after all, had placed in the garden of Eden, God had taken back the gift of immortality that he had initially given them. He cursed those whom he had so recently blessed. "Dust you are," he said in his fury, "and to dust you shall return." From that point on, neither the creator nor his creatures could look on the world and say without qualification "It is good."

This primeval defeat cast a shadow over God's defining victory over Pharaoh. What he gained by that victory he lost when, because of his own earlier curse, all those for whom he won the victory eventually died. By the same token, however, whatever God would lose by surrendering to Caesar would be recovered if he could lift his own curse and give the gift of eternal life to all those whom Caesar would kill.

By revoking the curse by which he had brought death into his world, God was able to swallow up his failure to act as a warrior against merely human foes in a larger victory over Satan, the enemy whose cunning had brought about not just the fall of humankind but also the fall of God himself. What is the plot of the Bible? John Milton, whom I reread with new respect late in the writing of these two books, put it with matchless brevity: *Paradise Lost, Paradise Regained.*

At a time like the present, when world war of a new sort threatens us all, our hope is for peace or, if war cannot be avoided, then for victory. Speaking personally, I find in the fear of war and in the flight from and pursuit of war a question that has held me in its grip since earliest childhood. My way of reading the Bible both in its Jewish edition, which I wrote about in *God: A Biography*, and in its Christian edition, which I write about in *Christ: A Crisis in the Life of God*, allows war in all its ramifications to become the central topic. Both editions allow God to win in the long run. Each in its own way tells God's story in a way that makes God's short-term defeat, even his utter absence from the battlefield, comprehensible. But one need not be either an observant Jew or a believing Christian to read and respond to either edition or either of these books of mine. It is enough to be a man or a woman, a boy or a girl, who has experienced the deep terror of the human condition and who craves a way to hear that terror tamed in language. Sister Mary Demetria tamed the terror for the frightened little boy I was in 1950. The Bible does it with greater pathos, greater violence, and greater exaltation for the adult that I have become, and for the little boy who still lives inside him.

Crucifixion and the Conscience of the West

JACK MILES*

All mankind is forgiven, but the Lord must die. This is the revolutionary import of the epilogue that, two thousand years ago, a group of radical Jewish writers appended to the sacred scripture of their religion. Because they did so, millions in the West today worship before the image of a deity executed as a criminal, and—no less important—other millions who never worship at all carry within their cultural DNA a religiously derived suspicion that somehow, someday, "the last will be first, and the first last" (Matt 20:1–6 KJV).

The crucifixion, the primal scene of Western religion and Western art, has lost much of its power to shock. At this late date, perhaps only a non-Western eye can truly see it. A Japanese artist now living in Los Angeles once recalled the horror most Japanese feel at seeing a corpse displayed as a religious icon, and of their further revulsion when the icon is explained to them. They ask, she said: "If he was so good, why did he die like that?" In Japanese culture, "good people end their lives with a good death, even a beautiful death, like the Buddha. Someone dying in such a hideous way— for us, he could only be a criminal."[1]

* Unless otherwise indicated, Scripture quotations in this chapter are from the author's own translation.

1. How strange it is that a scene of supreme ugliness should have become the supreme subject of Western art. Though there are many ways to make art of this subject, there is no way to make beauty of it; and its largest impact on Western art may consist of the space that it opened between the concept of art and the concept of beauty. Its inherent repugnance is ineradicable except perhaps by the aesthetic (or anaesthetic) expedient of displaying the cross without the crucified.

The reaction of a non-Christian Japanese to this icon is the correct reaction, then, yet it is worth recalling that the concepts of suicide and martyrdom, which diverged in

Her perception is correct. The crucifix is a violently obscene icon. To recover its visceral power, children of the twenty-first century must imagine a lynching, the body of the victim swollen and distorted, his head hanging askew above a broken neck, while the bystanders smile their twisted smiles. Then they must imagine that grisly spectacle reproduced at the holiest spot in whatever edifice they call holy. And yet to go even this far is still to miss the meaning of the image, for this victim is not just innocent: he is God Incarnate, the Lord himself in human form.

Winners usually look like winners, and losers like losers. But thanks to this paradoxical feature of the Christian myth, there remains lodged deep in the political consciousness of the West a readiness to believe that the apparent loser may be the real winner unrecognized. In Christianity's epilogue to the God story that it inherited from Judaism, the Lord God becomes human without ceasing to be the Lord and, unrecognized by all but a few, experiences the human condition at its worst before winning in the end a glorious victory. By losing to Caesar, he wins a duel with the devil and defeats death itself. The Bible ends as the greatest comedies so often end: with a solemn and festive wedding. The creator of a new heaven and a new earth in which every tear is wiped away becomes the spouse of the entire human race. By losing everything, God wins everything, for everybody, and the last word he speaks, with his bride at his side, is "Come!"

One of many implications of this epilogue to God's life story has been that in the West no regime can declare itself above review. All power is conditional; and when the powerless rise, God may be with them. The motif of divinity in disguise is not unique to Christianity; but the Christian motif of unrecognized divinity judicially tried, officially condemned, tortured by his captors, executed in public, buried, and only *then* rising from the dead and ascending into heaven is, if not literally unique, then at least unique in the breadth of its political influence. Every verse in "Sweet Little Jesus Boy," a black gospel tune sung at Christmas, ends with the wistful line "And they didn't know who he was." As his executioners nail him to the cross, Jesus prays: "Father, forgive them, for they know not what they do" (Luke 23:34 KJV). Wherever lines like these or the ideas behind them have spread,

the West after Augustine, have remained far less divergent in Japan. Though suicides in the eyes of the West, the kamikaze pilots of World War II were martyrs in the eyes of the Japanese; their deaths were understood to be not just heroic but also religiously sanctioned and supremely, artistically beautiful. Something very similar may be said of the Vietnamese Buddhist monks who immolated themselves during the Vietnam War; see Hearn, *Soldier and Monk.*

human authority has begun to lose its grip on unimpeachable legitimacy. In the West, any criminal may be Christ, and therefore any prosecutor Pilate. As the abolitionist poet James Russell Lowell put it:

> Truth forever on the scaffold, Wrong forever on the throne—
> Yet that scaffold sways the future, and, behind the dim unknown,
> Standeth God within the shadow, keeping watch above his own.[2]

The great Western myth is designed to raise a second, more profound and more disturbing question, however: if God had to suffer and die, then God had to inflict suffering and death upon himself. But why would God do this?

Tout comprendre, c'est tout pardonner, the French say: To understand everything is to forgive everything. Every perpetrator was first a victim. Behind every crime stretches a millennial history of earlier crimes, each in its way an extenuating circumstance. But to whom does this infinite regression lead in the end if not to God? The guilt of God is certainly not a Christian dogma, and yet it is an emotionally inescapable implication of the Christian myth, visible and audible in countless works of Christian art.[3] The pathos of those artistic enactments—those Masses and oratorios, passion plays and memorial liturgies, and above all those paintings and sculptures in which the unspeakable is left unspoken—is inseparable from the premise that God is inflicting this pain upon himself for a reason. "The real reason," as Albert Camus wrote in his haunting novel *The Fall*, "is that he himself knew he was not altogether innocent."[4]

A rural American folk hymn from the early nineteenth century captures this pathos in words of striking simplicity:

> What wondrous love is this, O my soul, O my soul?
> What wondrous love is this, O my soul?
> What wondrous love is this that caused the Lord of Bliss
> To bear the awful curse for my soul, for my soul,

2. Lowell, "Present Crisis," stanza 8.

3. To speak of the guilt of God or, as elsewhere in this book, of a wound in God or a crisis that God faces or a change that must and does occur in God is to open oneself to the charge of Gnosticism. But then Gnosticism—the ancient heresy in which, broadly, divinity and humanity save each other reciprocally—does not constitute a "charge" that can legitimately be brought against literary criticism. Theology may have a mandate to conform to the agreed-upon teaching of a church, even if not all who call themselves theologians accept that mandate. But there exists no church of literature in the first place, and therefore no true orthodoxy or heterodoxy in literary criticism.

4. Camus, *Fall*, 112.

To bear the awful curse for my soul?
To God and to the Lamb I will sing, I will sing,
To God and to the Lamb I will sing.
To God and to the Lamb who is the great I AM,
While millions join the theme, I will sing, I will sing,
While millions join the theme, I will sing.

"The great I AM" is, of course, God himself. The Lamb who is the great I AM is that same God turned into a sacrificial animal. The emotion the hymn is intended to evoke is rather like what many feel on visiting a battlefield where grave markers stretch to the far horizon. So many subjected to capital punishment, and so few, surely, guilty of anything approaching capital crime. Why had they to die? And did they die for me? *What wondrous love was this?*

Yet what brings tears to the eyes of some brings vomit to the mouths of others. For some, a military cemetery is a monument only to vanity and hypocrisy. For some, the crucifixion will ever be what it was for Friedrich Nietzsche in *The Antichrist:*

> *God on the cross*—are the horrible secret thoughts behind this symbol not understood yet? All that suffers, all that is nailed to the cross, is *divine.* All of us are nailed to the cross, consequently *we* are divine. We alone are divine. Christianity was a victory, a nobler outlook perished of it—Christianity has been the greatest misfortune of mankind so far.[5]

* * * * *

If Apollo and Dionysus are divine, then the brilliant and passionate are godlike. If the crucified Christ is divine, then the suffering are godlike. He is their ideal, and they pursue it through their own suffering. ("All of us are nailed to the cross, consequently *we* are divine.") Nietzsche found this dignification of suffering perverse, a wanton inversion of the natural order. Spiritually speaking, he said, the early Christians stank in his nostrils like Polish Jews.[6]

---

5. Nietzsche, *Portable Nietzsche,* 634; emphasis original. The phrase that Kaufmann translates as "the horrible secret thoughts" is, in Nietzsche's German, *die furchtbare Hintergedanldichkeit.* This is the phrase that I retranslate as "the frightening hidden premise" in the paragraph immediately following on this page. See Nietzsche, *Antichrist,* 232.

6. "One does well to put on gloves when reading the New Testament. The proximity

Nietzsche's visceral reaction, like his visceral anti-Semitism, commonly prompts a visceral counterreaction, but by this visceral intensity on both sides we may measure the power of what he was reacting against in the first place. His reaction was not gratuitous. He had seen, and seen correctly, something utterly shocking at the heart of the Christian myth, a "frightening hidden premise" to which the genteel Christianity of the late nineteenth century had grown numb. And he was prepared to offer a shocking anti-myth in order to make the original horror visible again. In *The Antichrist*, written in the last months before he lost his mind, Nietzsche asked:

> What is good? Everything that heightens the feeling of power in man, the will to power, power itself.
> What is bad? Everything that is born of weakness.
> What is happiness? The feeling that power is *growing*, that resistance is overcome.
> Not contentedness but more power; not peace but war; not virtue but fitness (Renaissance virtue, *virtù*, virtue unadulterated by morality).
> The weak and the failures shall perish: first principle of *our* love of man. And they shall even be given every possible assistance.
> What is more harmful than any vice? Active pity for all the failures and all the weak: Christianity.[7]

* * * * *

As we look back on a century of genocide, the sarcasm of "And they shall even be given every possible assistance" is ghastly, even as rhetoric. And yet the larger point is powerfully made. The divinization of the victim is the wellspring of revolution, even as the demonization of the victim is the wellspring of repression.

To Christianity's "the last shall be first," somnolently intoned from countless German pulpits, Nietzsche reacts—like a madman in the back pew—with outraged astonishment. The last first! Why should the *first* not be first? Do they not deserve it? What have the last done that they should displace the first? *Leave the losers at the bottom where they belong!* The

---

of so much uncleanliness almost forces one to do this. We would no more choose the 'first Christians' to associate with than Polish Jews—not that one even required any objection to them: they both do not smell good" (*Antichrist*, in Nietzsche, *Portable Nietzsche*, 625, §46). The first of these two sentences is often quoted; the last, never.

7. Nietzsche, *Antichrist*, 572; emphasis original.

madman's outburst disrupts the church service, but the opening outrage, in truth, was that verse droned from the pulpit. The madman's offense was to take it seriously, as a statement that, if it could not be accepted, would have to be forcefully rejected. And the ushers who struggle to subdue the madman must struggle as well, if they are sincere Christians, with their human, all too human, tendency to agree with him.

Can there be such a thing as innocent, fully human suffering? Do not all adults have a little something on their consciences? Paradoxically, perhaps, humans believe more spontaneously in the innocence of animals than they do in their own. On a visit to Turin some months after writing *The Antichrist*, Nietzsche, long on the brink of insanity, was driven over the brink by the spectacle of a horse being flogged savagely by a coachman. The distraught philosopher flung himself on the fallen beast, wrapping his arms around its neck, seeking in vain to defend it. From the asylum where he was taken, he wrote his last semi-coherent letter, signing it "The Crucified," and then sank irretrievably into the madness that would last until his death a decade later.

That helpless horse has everything to do with Nietzsche's obsession with the crucifixion and no little to do with the tenacity of the Christian myth in minds less susceptible to it than his. Ancient Israel felt toward the lamb the sensitivity that modern Europeans typically feel toward the horse. Hyper-domesticated, like the human animal itself, and therefore poignantly vulnerable to abuse, the lamb invited metaphorical use in myth and ritual. Thus, in the book of Exodus, the blood of the Passover lamb saved the Israelites from the angel of death whom God had sent against Egypt. Smeared on the lintels of the Israelites, this blood warned the angel that these were the houses he must "pass over" on his awful errand. In the book of Isaiah, several centuries later, reference was made to a mysterious servant who, like a lamb, suffered without protest. In the Acts of the Apostles, this lamb is identified as the divine Christ, who has shed (and shared) his blood to save all mankind not from any passing threat but from mortality itself:

An Ethiopian had been on a pilgrimage to Jerusalem. He was a eunuch, an officer at the court of the *kandake*, or queen, of Ethiopia, her chief treasurer. On his way home, he sat in his chariot reading the prophet Isaiah. The Spirit said to Philip, "Catch up with that chariot." When Philip ran up, he heard him reading Isaiah the prophet aloud and asked, "Do you understand what you are reading?" He replied, "How can I, with no one to explain it to me?" But he urged Philip to get in and take the seat next to him. Now the passage of scripture he was reading was this:

> Like a lamb led to the slaughterhouse,
> Like a sheep dumb before its shearers,
> He never opens his mouth.
> In his humiliation fair judgment is denied him,
> His descendants—who will ever speak of them,
> Since his life on earth has been cut short?

The eunuch turned to Philip and said, "Tell me, is the prophet referring to himself or someone else?" Starting, therefore, with this text of scripture, Philip proceeded to explain the good news of Jesus to him.

Farther down the road they came to a body of water, and the eunuch said, "Look, here is some water; is there anything to prevent my being baptized?" He ordered the chariot to stop; then Philip and the eunuch both went down into the water, and he baptized him (Acts 8:27–38; passage in italics from Isaiah 53:7–8).

The atrocity of castration burns behind the lines that the eunuch is reading. Was he shorn of his testicles when he was just a lamb? Did he open his mouth before the shearers? In his humiliation was fair judgment denied him? And who will ever speak of his descendants? When he asks (in what tone of voice?) "Is the prophet referring to himself or someone else?" whom does he have in mind?

We do not know, but how can we refrain from guessing? It was a subtle but powerful literary move on Luke's part to make Christianity's first convert outside Palestine a black eunuch and to give him just these verses to read.[8] The enslaved eunuch is, if you will, just the kind of convert Nietzsche would have predicted, believing as he did that Christianity is a religion for slaves and other emasculated losers, a cult of resentment deriving all its malignant energy from their bad luck. And yet, so far as we can tell, Philip says nothing to the eunuch about the eunuch's own suffering, only directing his attention to the sufferings of the prophesied Lamb of God. What this kindles in the man, however, is a desire to undergo the death

---

8. The Ethiopian, a diaspora Jew, is reading the Jewish scriptures in Greek, for the verses quoted translate the Septuagint, the pre-Christian Greek edition of the Jewish scriptures. The Septuagint differs from the Masoretic, the surviving Hebrew text of the Tanakh, in a way suggesting that certain passages must have been translated from a variant Hebrew original. This passage from Isaiah may be one such. See appendix 1 [in Miles's *Christ*] on the importance of the Septuagint in Christian exegesis and in the genesis of the Bible.

and resurrection rite of baptism, uniting his humiliation with God's own and trusting that it will lead to exaltation in just the way that so appalled Nietzsche.

Castration is an atrocity within an atrocity. Perhaps someone in Ethiopia could have been hunted down and punished for castrating Philip's convert, but who can be punished for perpetrating the human condition itself? To use the language of the myth, who is to be blamed for our expulsion from Eden? It is the Lord himself who cursed what he created. "Dust you are, and to dust you shall return," he swore (Gen 3:19), bringing death into a world that, until that moment, had known only life. That was the curse, but can we make him bear it? Our offense was so mild, his punishment so ferocious. Can we avenge ourselves upon him?

No, we cannot; we cannot make him "bear the awful curse" that he has inflicted on his creatures. But he can make himself bear it. And when he does, all lesser offenses can be caught up in one primal offense, his own, for which, though not without a wrenching change in his character, he can wreak the ultimate vengeance upon himself and deliver the ultimate gift—eternal life—as atonement.[9] In the words of Paul (2 Cor 5:19), he can "reconcile the world to himself" and himself to the world. As God, the Lord cannot cease to exist; but as Christ, he can taste death. Betrayed and abandoned, he can breathe his last breath in pain. The myth that he once did so has within it, as the greatest literature always does, the power to still that rage against the universe which any individual history can engender.

* * * * *

It doesn't take castration, after all, to raise the question. It doesn't take genocide. Far, far smaller misfortunes easily suffice. Cesare Pavese, a brilliant poet dead by his own hand at the age of forty-two, wrote, famously: "No

---

9. "Atonement" in Christian theology ordinarily refers to atonement by Christ to God for the sins of mankind. Atonement theology, though its roots are medieval, had a particularly long and active history in American Protestantism through the nineteenth and into the twentieth century. See T. Jenkins, *Character of God*. A German Protestant theologian not afraid to speak of the suffering of God as God is Jürgen Moltmann. See Moltmann, *Crucified God*. Yet this notion, though more generously accommodated in such contemporary theology than when it was dismissed as the "patripassionist" heresy, lives on even now principally in the informal, unregulated rest of the Christian tradition—which is to say in its literature, its music, and its art. For a striking confrontation of Christian art and Protestant atonement theology, see Altizer, "Protestant Jesus."

one ever lacks a good reason for suicide." He did not mean to trivialize the act, only to suggest that we refrain from it, more than we realize, by selective inattention to sorrows that, dwelt upon, would undercut our will to live. The myth and, especially, the ritual of the crucified God are ways to bring those sorrows, those horrors, to mind without succumbing to them. What they take away is not guilt, divine or human, but anger, not the sin of the past but the still uncommitted sin of the future.

In Louis Begley's novel *Mistler's Exit*, a wealthy American advertising executive impulsively flies to Venice to see again some of his favorite Titians. A young woman whom he meets in his hotel accompanies him on his visit to the great painter's *Martyrdom of Saint Lawrence*, but he surprises her—and perhaps himself—with his sarcasm about it. "I haven't noticed," he says,

> that it's a part of religious iconography to have the Father or the Son attend torture sessions of the martyrs. In fact, right now I can't think of any painting of the crucifixion or the deposition where the Father or the Holy Ghost looks on . . . One wonders why. Celestial squeamishness? Or is it respect for the logic of the faithful? Fear that belief might be strained beyond the breaking point if the Father actually observed such things being done to the Son and did nothing to stop them?[10]

Mistler is not the connoisseur he thinks he is. Medieval and Renaissance art frequently portrayed the Father, garbed as a priest, holding the transverse beam of the cross in his own hands, as if displaying the suffering Son to the viewer, while the Spirit, in the form of a dove, hovers near. All these paintings illustrate the perfect identity of the Father and the Son at the climax of the Son's agony. A celebrated example is Masaccio's *The Holy Trinity with the Virgin and Saint John*, in which the Father elevates the body of the Son above an altar just as, in the Mass, the priest elevates the consecrated bread, the sacramental body of Christ, above an altar.[11] "This is my

10. Begley, *Mistler's Exit*, 92.

11. The fact that Masaccio portrays the Trinity above an altar and inside a chapel whose architecture is part of the painting may suggest that the painting was not, in fact, an altarpiece. However, the meaning of the work is the same in either case. Art historian John Shearman writes that the altar shown below the chapel in the painting "is a part of its meaning, in that the antetype [of the chapel] in the Old Testament, the Tabernacle of the Covenant, had an altar outside it; but this is a fiction of an altar, and fictions cannot be consecrated. I think there is no good evidence of a real altar to which the fresco served as *dossale*; and a real altar seems rendered redundant by the fiction. For that reason the

body" is, in effect, the silent caption of the painting, but the words are the Father's, not the Son's, for it is he, not the Son, who looks outward at the viewer. The suffering of the Son and the suffering of the Father are one as the Father and the Son are one with the Spirit in—recalling the title of the painting—the Trinity.

In Begley's novel, Mistler's young companion does not know that he is dying of cancer. The martyred saint and the crucified savior are psychological surrogates. The death Mistler wants God to notice is his own, and his deepest grievance, to quote the psychologist Allen Wheelis, is his "awareness that, before we die, nothing is going to happen. That big vague thing, that redemptive fulfillment, is an illusion, a beckoning bribe to keep us loyal. A symphony has a climax, a poem builds to a burst of meaning, but we are unfinished business. No coming together of strands. The game is called because of darkness."[12] Mistler does not believe in God, but his rage that the big vague thing is not going to happen is so huge and so personally felt that he craves the vindication of repudiating the God in whom he does not believe. Moreover, were it only possible, he would willingly take a step beyond repudiation and punish God.

But what if he were looking at a painting in which, if he chose to see it so, he could see God being punished for Mistler's death? What sort of difference would that make? Subliminally, paintings by artists like Masaccio, El Greco, and Titian have stilled the rage in many Mistlers, but what finds its way to the painters' canvases can be found as well in an artistically alert reading of the scriptures that inspired them. Such is the reading—a reading of the New Testament as a work of imaginative literature—that this book will attempt.

Paradise Lost, Paradise Regained: the English language may never surpass John Milton's four-word summary of the Bible. But there is another way to "justify the ways of God to man," as Milton aspired to do, than by granting God blanket immunity and then bowdlerizing his testimony lest he incriminate himself. An interpretation of the Bible in which God is allowed to be more hero than saint and in which it is taken for granted that no hero is without his flaw, not even the hero of a divine comedy, is the kind that, if a new Milton ever arose, could yield a new biblical epic.

Trinity is not strictly an altarpiece. But because it is one virtually, it had a great effect upon the way artists thought about altarpieces, nowhere more than in Venice" (Shearman, *Only Connect*, 66).

12. Wheelis, *Listener*, 210.

Dios escribe derecho con líneas torcidas: God writes straight with crooked lines. The first, spoken pathos of the crucifix as an icon—that the crucified is both innocent and divine—yields to a second, unspoken pathos: that he is both divine and guilty. He is guilty less of sin than of ignorance. At the start, he was ignorant of his own power: he had to discover it by using it and by misusing it. Later, he was blind to his own weakness: That, too, he had to discover by succumbing to it. At length, he chose to undergo a human death in order both to prove to himself and to reveal to the world the full, mixed truth about himself the truth that the horrified Nietzsche could only denounce.

Jesus bore, ironically, the name of the greatest warrior of his people. That we call him Jesus is an accident of Latin translation. *Iēsous* in the original Greek of the Gospels translates Hebrew *yehoshua`* or *yeshua`*, alternate forms of the name Joshua, a name compounded of Hebrew words meaning "the Lord is salvation." But how can this Joshua save others if he cannot save himself?

As the time for his execution draws near, God gives his answer to that question in a poem that includes the lines

> Unless a grain of wheat falls into the earth and dies,
> it remains but a single grain.
> Yet if it dies, it yields a rich harvest.
> (John 12:24)

* * * * *

The grain that must fall into the earth and die is the divine identity itself, which must be violently revised: "This is the very reason why I have come to this hour." As he hangs in agony, they say of him, "He saved others, himself he cannot save" (Mark 15:31 KJV). The irony is not in their mouths. They speak, as they imagine, the simple truth. The irony is in our ears, and in his.

The world is a great crime, and someone must be made to pay for it. Mythologically read, the New Testament is the story of how someone, the right someone, does pay for it. The ultimately responsible party accepts his responsibility. And once he has paid the price, who else need be blamed, who else need be punished? The same act that exposes all authority as provisional renders all revenge superfluous. And because the death of God does this, it functions within the myth as not just another death but a redemptive death, one that saves us from the violence that we might otherwise feel justified in inflicting on one another. God must die, yes, but he will rise, and at his empty tomb, where none is king, all may be forgiven and may submit to one another. Thus does his kingdom come. Thus does the Lamb of God take away the sin of the world.

8

What Did Jesus Contribute
to Western Philosophy?

LESZEK KOŁAKOWSKI (1927–2009) WAS a Polish philosopher and historian of ideas. During World War II, his father was burned alive by Nazi occupiers. Young Leszek became an ardent member of the Communist Party and an atheist. In his twenties, he was already recognized as one of the most brilliant thinkers of his generation, and the Soviet Union invited him to Moscow in 1950 to view its Communism in action. Kołakowski was not impressed, writing of the "material and spiritual desolation" he witnessed. Through his subsequent critiques, Kołakowski became a kind of guru of anti-Communism on both sides of the Iron Curtain.

Increasingly dismissive of secular materialism, he became convinced that religion is a necessary component of our lives. He was fascinated by Christianity in particular. In 1965, he published in Polish the monumental study *Religious Consciousness and Church Bonding: Studies in Non-denominational Christianity in the Seventeenth Century*.[1] This magnum opus brought to life a diverse array of little-known European thinkers who embraced Christian ideas but radically rejected affiliation with any existing church. "In opposition to the Church's 'law,' they all favored a religion of direct 'grace.'"[2]

---

1. This is the English title; alas, the book has been translated into French but not English: Kołakowski, *Świadomość religijna*.

2. Billington, "Leszek Kolakowski," para. 12.

Kołakowski later taught at Oxford, Yale, Chicago, and Berkeley. In 2003, he was the inaugural winner of the Library of Congress's million-dollar John W. Kluge Prize for the Study of Humanity.

DISCUSSION QUESTIONS

Kołakowski says Jesus passed along "precepts which were genuinely new and which—crucially—remain vital not as abstract norms but as living principles."[3]

    a. Abolishing law in favor of love. "Again, this must be stressed: *abolishing*, not supplementing."[4]

    b. The hope of eliminating violence from human relations

    c. Man shall not live by bread alone.

    d. The abolition of the idea of a chosen people

    e. The essential wretchedness of the temporal world[5]

1. Think about these five principles in your own life. Which one of them seems the strangest and most alien to you? Why?

2. Which of these five is closest to a "living principle" in your life?

3. Which of the five do you hope will play an even bigger role in your life?

4. Kołakowski concludes:

> The person and the teaching of Jesus Christ cannot be invalidated or removed from our culture if that culture is to continue to exist and to create itself. . . . For he incarnated, in his person, the ability to express one's own truth fully and loudly, to defend it to the end with no evasion, and to resist to the end the pressure of established reality which rejected him. He taught how we can confront the world and ourselves without resorting to violence. He was a model of that radical authenticity to which, uniquely, every human being can give true life to his own values.[6]

    How does "radical authenticity" relate to your life?

3. Kołakowski, "Jesus Christ," this vol., 138.
4. Kołakowski, "Jesus Christ," this vol., 139.
5. Kołakowski, "Jesus Christ," this vol., 139–42.
6. Kołakowski, "Jesus Christ," this vol., 144.

Jesus Christ—Prophet and Reformer

LESZEK KOŁAKOWSKI

When a historian deals with Jesus, he is interested above all in what can reliably be said about this man, in what we know about him for sure. He also wants to know about the antecedents of his teachings in Jewish culture, and how the image of the Jewish God changed from the Pentateuch to the late prophets, and whether Jesus the prophet can be taken as a continuation or crowning of those changes. He is interested in the results of research on the Qumran manuscripts and the light they have shed on the problem. These are topics that can be profitably discussed only by specialists, and they are not what I want to discuss here.

A historian of ideas may also want to situate Jesus in the whole history of Christianity, exploring, in his research on this inexhaustible topic, the boundless area of thought and events which grew up around the myth of Christ. Indeed, it is difficult, when speaking about Jesus the man, to shake off the twenty centuries of events through which we *see* him. The figure of Jesus is enveloped in the shadow of theology and in the thicket of theological controversies that surrounds every word of the Gospels. How can we ignore the vast areas of ambiguity, real or ostensible, with which the history of Christianity has weighed down the teachings of its founder? But this, too, is not what concerns me here.

A historian of religion may treat Jesus as an element in a certain mythological structure, which he might compare with others in order to bring out cultural differences and similarities. He may, although this is difficult, try to ignore the extent to which the figure of Jesus is enveloped in the shadow of the contemporary world and the presence of Christianity in it; he may aspire to the same degree of disinterestedness and objectivity the same scholarly and aesthetic distance, that we display toward Egyptian or Greek myths. But this is also not what I want to attempt here.

Finally, a biographer may try to unravel the psychology of Jesus and put together a consistent psychological profile of the whole person—if he can free himself from all ulterior motives, whether apologetic and Christian or blasphemous and anti-Christian. But this, too, is not what interests me here.

What interests me is the purely philosophical point of view: a view, in other words, that is neither historical nor psychological nor that of the historian of religion. My aim is to attain enough mental freedom to read the canonical and apocryphal texts of the Gospels without recalling the commentaries, or even the Epistles of St. Paul; to read just the simple words, without reading any complex theological or philosophical speculations into them. I would like to summarize what the layman can discern in the figure and teaching of Jesus: the layman who professes no particular Christian faith, embraces no dogma and belongs to no church community, but who does feel himself to belong to the larger tradition of which Christianity is an essential part—the tradition of which Buddha, Socrates, Kant, and Marx are also a part. I do not want to reconstruct the psychological profile of Jesus. I am interested in his place within the European tradition as a whole: in how, and in which of its aspects, the mission he ascribed to himself became a component of the intricately woven tapestry which makes up our cultural heritage. And I am interested in this tradition independently of the christological dogmas around which the Christian religious consciousness has been shaped.

PHILOSOPHERS AND JESUS

Jesus Christ was not, as we know, a philosopher. Textbooks on religious philosophy, even Christian textbooks, do not mention him, and modern philosophers rarely deal with him. However, some philosophers have done so, and it is worth mentioning some of their views in order to outline the various types of philosophical approaches to this extraordinary figure.

Of the great philosophers, Pascal, Kierkegaard, Hegel, Nietzsche, and Jaspers wrote about Jesus. For Hegel, he represented a phase of human historical self-knowledge; he was a concrete, sensory manifestation of that idea of God at which man arrives when he conceives of God as something in which he participates—something of which he himself is a manifestation, another form of being. Thus the person of Jesus is almost reduced to a stage of human self-consciousness in its relation to the absolute. This does not mean that Hegel makes Jesus unreal, stripping him of personhood and humanity; he acknowledges that Jesus is far more human than the Greek anthropomorphic gods. But he deprives Jesus of his peculiar extra-historical uniqueness; of that quality—that timeless exceptionality, at once singular and enduring—which established Christianity and which is embedded in the belief that here was something supranatural that irrupted into history from outside it.

Kierkegaard, on this issue as on others, developed his own view in opposition to Hegel, depicting Christ as always contemporary, and true for Christians only by virtue of this contemporaneousness. Christ, he said, is no more than a sterile item of historical information for us if we see him as the transmitter of a *past* revelation; he is the real Christian life for each individual only when that individual is able to make him *literally* contemporary and thus to understand his invitation—"Come unto me, all ye that labor and are heavy laden, and I will give you rest"—as addressed to him personally, always valid and spoken to him anew at every moment. For a Christian, Jesus is not just a messiah who appeared at a certain historical moment to teach dogmas or preach commandments in God's name. He is the personal embodiment of the permanence of Christianity in every individual Christian; an ever-vital counter element of every existence; a presence in which each existence will seek the answer to its own frailty and its own wretchedness.

Pascal's attitude to Jesus, most evident in his attacks on deism and the "philosophers' God," was, despite all the differences, basically the same. For Pascal, the world manifests neither the complete absence nor the evident presence of a deity; it is not utterly abandoned by God, nor is it obviously under his protection. It manifests "the presence of a God who is hidden." This ambiguity of God's presence in the world is the ambiguity of our fate: the fate of those who are able to know God but who are permanently tainted by sin. It is through Jesus Christ that our knowledge of God becomes for us the knowledge of our own wretchedness, and we need this conjoined knowledge. We can learn each of these two truths—that God exists and that we are wretched—separately, but only the apprehension of Jesus as a person amalgamates them and contains them, necessarily, as one joint truth. By itself, our knowledge of our infirmity is a source of despair; by itself, our knowledge of God is merely speculative, theoretical, without value in our lives. But in the apprehension of Jesus we attain at once the full awareness of our fall and the hope of a possible cure; and it is this that constitutes Christian faith. Thus a purely philosophical Christianity, based on speculative proofs, is not possible. Nor is a purely historical one, based on what we know from the Bible. Jesus Christ appears to us not just in his dogmatic and his historical aspects, but as a real existence, a real redeemer; and it is through this presence, which is neither simply a fact nor simply a doctrine, that we become aware both of the darkness in which we live and of the way which leads out of that darkness.

Finally, Nietzsche's is also one of the "great" philosophical interpretations of the figure of Christ. Nietzsche is the greatest of those very few who have dared to proclaim themselves not only enemies of Christianity but enemies of Christ. For him, Jesus was someone who wanted to annihilate all the important values of life, who glorified his own inability to resist and who raised this weakness to the rank of a virtue. He robbed all values of their reality by transferring them to man's spiritual "interior," and he codified a morality for those who cannot defend their own rights and who seek comfort in their own passivity making it a cause for pride.

These attitudes, briefly sketched, are three ways in which philosophers have approached the person of Jesus. Nietzsche addresses him as one prophet to another; as a true prophet to a false one. Hegel's approach is that of a historian of the spirit toward a certain historical phase. Pascal and Kierkegaard approach him as Christians who seek the supranatural realities of their faith in its most personal values. In some limited sense, Pascal's and Kierkegaard's approach may be acceptable to those who are not bound by the dogmatic content of Christianity. Not, of course, in the sense that they see Christ is a personal and historically unequivocal embodiment of the supranatural world, to whom they could address their questions or worries, but in the sense that Jesus, like all great thinkers, prophets, reformers and philosophers, has that peculiar contemporaneous-ness which can be achieved where universal values spring from one unique source. A philosopher, if he wants to go beyond the purely historical or purely factual point of view, will not approach a philosophical or religious tradition as a fact that is simply there to be understood, nor as a line of thought which is simply to be agreed or disagreed with; he will not view a cultural tradition as a cumulation of "truths," nor as a sequence of historically neutralized facts. He will try rather, to bring out those of its values which are universal and yet enduringly linked to their author, inextricably bound up with their personal source. This duality is one of the more difficult elements of the philosophical approach to tradition. Jesus, on this approach, is reducible neither to a set of events (a set that would also comprise the content of his teaching) nor to a set of abstract values that could be viewed and assessed quite independently of the circumstances in which they came into being. We approach his teaching as, to use an ugly expression, "essentialized fact," or as a universal value whose content is linked to its historical origin.

JESUS' MAIN PROPHECY

From a purely historical perspective, Jesus was a Jew from Galilee who believed in the Jewish God and believed that this God had entrusted him with a special mission of teaching. He was also someone of whom his disciples in turn believed that he could calm winds by his command, walk across a lake, draw fish into nets, resurrect the dead, heal lepers, make the blind see again, drive out demons from the possessed, talk with Moses and Elijah, multiply bread for the poor, and turn water into wine and wine into blood; they also believed that he fulfilled the promises of the Old Testament about the Messiah and that his mission was attested to by his resurrection. This Jesus, although he accepted the tribute of his believers, did not consider himself to be God; indeed he denied that he could be so considered. When he was called good he said that only God is good; he acknowledged that he did not know when the promised day would come; he said, "Not what I will, but what thou wilt." In this sense one cannot say that Jesus made Christianity, if the belief in his divinity is counted among Christianity's fundamental precepts. It was Paul who began the deification process, and in the end, in spite of the opposition which still persisted among the pre-Nicene fathers, he prevailed; thus was the dominant understanding of Christianity definitively established, despite numerous "Arian" relapses. This Jesus considered himself, we may assume, a Jewish reformer, charged with a supranatural mission as God's anointed, that is, as Christ, who brought from God—the same God in whom he and his listeners believed—the news of the approaching end of the world and an appeal to all to prepare themselves immediately for the final cataclysm. He was convinced that the end of the world was imminent—so imminent that he sometimes told his listeners and disciples that many of them would see the coming of God's kingdom on earth with their own eyes. This coming would be preceded by famines, pestilence, and earthquakes, by falling stars and the eclipse of the sun, and would end with the visible descent of God's son from the heavens, surrounded by angels playing trumpets. The failure of these prophecies to be fulfilled did not weaken the belief of the disciples, who explained them differently. But the expectation of imminent catastrophe imposed an entirely new perspective on things: from that moment on, all worldly concerns disappear in the shadow of the apocalypse. Earthly realities, the whole multiplicity of things that are important in life, lose all meaning and all independent value. The material world is no longer important: it can still be, it still is, an object of duty, but it could not be an object of desire, for in its fragility it was approaching its end.

JESUS THE REFORMER

In this light, the precepts of the new teaching, and the extent to which it really was new, can be understood.

Readers of the Gospels have long been struck by certain inconsistencies in the personality of Jesus. He preaches peace, forgiveness, mercy and nonresistance to evil; but in his own behavior he is quick to anger and easily irritated, even by small things. He warns that he will send away even those who perform miracles, prophesy, and exorcize demons in his name, and deny that he ever knew them, if they do not fulfill the will of God. He says that a terrible vengeance will befall cities which do not believe in him, and promises that on the day of judgment the fate of Tyre and Sidon will be more tolerable than that of Chorazin and Bethsaida, which disregarded his teachings in spite of his miracles. To Peter, when he expresses the hope that his Lord will not be killed, he says, "Get thee behind me, Satan." He curses a fig tree on which he finds no fruit and condemns it to wither away, although it is not the right time of year for figs. He drives out the money changers from the temple with a scourge. He proclaims that he brings not peace but a sword, that he will separate families and that because of him in every house fathers shall be set at variance against sons and daughters against mothers. His listeners say, "These are hard sayings." Opposition or skepticism rouse him to violent anger. He is unshakably certain of his mission, and it is only at the very last moment, as he is dying in torment, that he seems to burst out with a cry of despair to the God who has forsaken him. But even that cry of despair is a quotation from the psalmist.

It may seem that the impulsive character of Jesus does not quite fit his teaching; some of his behavior seems to reveal the anger of the old Jewish

God whose image he changes in his teaching (which was, in fact, in accordance with the intentions of earlier prophets).

And indeed it is difficult to sum up in one word Jesus' attitude toward the Old Testament—a difficulty testified to by the endless disputes on the matter in the history of Christianity (Did he abolish the law of the Old Testament? Supplement it? Amend it?). The Sermon on the Mount begins with the statement that he does not want to destroy the law but to fulfill it; but what follows is hard to reconcile with that passage. When Jesus broadens the commandment against killing to encompass mere anger, and the commandment against adultery to encompass mere lust, we may consider him to be supplementing the laws, in the same spirit that guides the whole of his teaching: it is not actions that matter but the spirit from which they spring, not behavior but purity of heart and love of one's neighbor with no ulterior motive. But when he contrasts the principle of an eye for an eye with refraining from resistance to evil and turning the other cheek, he is no longer just supplementing the Old Testament: he is abolishing it, apparently without noticing. He certainly does not want to break the continuity of the Jewish creed; he wants to renew it and "internalize" it. He disregards the Jewish laws of ritual; he does not observe the Sabbath, nor perform ritual ablutions; he does not pay taxes to the Jewish cult, which outrages the orthodox. He represents a continuity with the late prophets, but evokes the rigorous laws of Deuteronomy as if deliberately to stress the contrast between his own teaching and the old tradition (which by then was of course partly out of date). The break in the continuity was achieved by his disciples, mainly in the Jewish diaspora. But it was not just the news of his miraculous resurrection that created the break, but also his teaching, which can easily be formulated so that it no longer merely supplements the faith of Israel but transgresses it in a fundamental way. And indeed this is how St. Paul views the matter.

This is a crucial point, and it means that Jesus does not, in fact, so much replace some laws by others, complete them or amend them, as teach that laws are not needed at all, for love entails the command, and thus makes it superfluous; it is, so to speak, spontaneously bound up with it. And only love is important. In other words, the contractual relation between man and God is not altered by a change in the content of the contract, but ceases to exist entirely, and is supplanted by a relation of love. This is how Paul understood Christ's teaching, and Augustine, and Luther. Only that which comes from love has true value, and whatever springs from love cannot be judged by laws nor measured by a paragraph in a decree. No action matters unless it springs from a desire to do God's will. We all have duties toward the world, but no rights: no claims on it and no right to expect anything from it. Never before in Mediterranean culture had the principle of this fundamental dichotomy been stated so starkly, and it was expressed with great force: the soul and the will to do good on the one hand, the rest of the world and the totality of existing things on the other. Only the soul matters. In view of the approaching catastrophe, only a blind man would take comfort from his temporal achievements. The kingdom of heaven is a priceless pearl for which we must abandon all we possess, all our goods. "For what is a man profited, if he shall gain the whole world, and lose his own soul?"

The mission of Jesus Christ is to reveal the wretchedness of the temporal world. "Freely ye have received, freely give. Provide neither gold, nor silver, nor brass in your purses, nor scrip for your journey, neither two coats, neither shoes, nor yet staves." All temporal bonds, all that links us to the physical world, is reduced to nothing before that single truly important bond: the bond with God. The rest is secondary—either indifferent or hostile. Jesus renounces his mother and brothers, saying that his disciples are his family; he demands that his followers abandon their fathers and mothers, wives and children, sisters and brothers, in his name. According to Luke he even demands that they hate their fathers, mothers, brothers, sisters, and children.

In the world Jesus reveals there is no gradation between good and evil. It is divided into the chosen and the cast out, the sheep and the goats, the heirs of life and the victims of eternal fire, the sons of the kingdom and the sons of evil, good seeds and weeds. To him who has, will be given; from him who has not, even that which he has will be taken away. There is nothing in between. This division corresponds exactly to the division between the spirit of love and the spirit of lust. To be sure, Jesus speaks to everyone: he says that he has come to call sinners, not the righteous, to repentance; he asks that faults be forgiven up to seventy-seven times; he believes that the repentant heart will wash away sin. But at the same time he knows very well that he cannot break obdurate pride. He hates the proud, the powerful, the self-assured, the smug and self-satisfied with their privileges and power, the rich and the avaricious; to them he does not promise the kingdom. He embraces the despised and the wretched, prostitutes and tax collectors; they believe in him because they know that temporal life is misery and suffering, and this is what one must believe in order to accept and understand Jesus' teaching.

The dichotomy between the world and God's kingdom is a radical one. It is also a complete reversal of all values: the despised are raised to glory, while the proud are cast out with contempt. This division is the second point which marks a crucial departure from the traditional Jewish view of the world. It is a universal division and uniquely important, unconnected to the division into the chosen people and the rest. Here, too, Jesus perhaps wanted to be only a renewer of the Judaic tradition, not its destroyer; here, too, he was building on foundations laid by the prophets. But in choosing its older and more radical form, he was opposing the tradition; by confronting his own teaching with classical Jewish law, he brought out the conflict between the two, and abolished the idea of the chosen people, introducing, in its place, a universal principle of division.

All these novelties were generalized, so to speak, by his disciples, above all by Paul. In his writings, law and faith are opposed; the principle of universalism is unequivocally formulated (for God "there is neither Jew nor Greek"); the wretchedness of temporal life becomes an injunction to asceticism. At the same time, however, and in the very same epistles, the new division became established as a dogma: condemnations of heretics began to appear. The death of Jesus cemented the reform and produced a separatist community: Christianity as a community was founded not on the disciples' belief in the truth of Jesus' teaching, but on their belief in his resurrection, and later in his divinity And although in the later history of Christianity the deification of Christ—which is not confirmed in the Gospels—was sometimes questioned, even the doubters acknowledged that the only common dogma of Christianity as such, Christianity without further specification, was the belief that Jesus is Christ, that he was a historical figure, a man born in Galilee and crucified in Jerusalem, and that he is God's anointed. This dogma was constitutive of Christianity even in its "loosest" variants.

But Jesus remains alive in our culture not only for those who believe in his divinity or even just in his supranatural mission. He is present in our culture not through the dogmas of this or that religious community but through the value of certain precepts which were genuinely new and which—crucially—remain vital not as abstract norms but as living principles, enduringly bound up with his name and his life as handed down by tradition and quite independently of that tradition's historical accuracy.

JESUS FOR US

Let us summarize these new rules—rules which can stand independently of Jesus' apocalyptic prophecies and of the belief in the imminent end of the world, although we know that in his teaching they were a function of those prophecies. They may be summarized in five points:

1. *Abolishing law in favor of love.* Again, this must be stressed: *abolishing*, not supplementing. This idea entered European culture as the belief that human relations which are based on trust cancel or preclude contractual relations: if harmonious coexistence is based on mutual trust and love, there is no need for contractual claims and duties. When the God of the Pentateuch—a vengeful God, who demanded obedience, sometimes cruel obedience; a God who made the covenant with Abraham for the price of absolute submission, the readiness even to sacrifice one's only child—when this God was transformed into the God of mercy, a new way of viewing human relations was opened. The opposition between contractual relations and relations of love has remained alive in our culture in innumerable varieties, as something that, while genetically connected with Christian beliefs, is not organically bound to them. What is the opposition between "existential" and "pragmatic" communication in contemporary philosophy but a recreation of this distinction? For it was not only Christian philosophies that continued to recreate this opposition. It is recreated anew in the philosophy of Rousseau, of Kierkegaard, and of Jaspers. And when Marx contrasts the relations of interest that obtain in a society based on the exchange of goods with the relations of free association that obtain between people who are voluntarily bound by mutual solidarity, he, too, is recreating the same idea, taking it up, in turn, from the old socialists. It is an idea which is rooted in Jesus, but which in modern Christianity appears most often in heresies and most rarely in the Church. Even Nietzsche, when he says that whatever flows from love is beyond good and evil, is repeating, unbeknownst to himself, the idea of the enemy. All utopias which want to abolish contractual and legal bonds in favor of voluntary and genuinely experienced solidarity, in short all utopias of universal brotherhood, flower from the same root, however indifferent they may be to their own remote origins.

2. *The hope of eliminating violence from human relations.* This is a hope that often seems to us to be particularly utopian and naive. Indeed, we can say with no hesitation that we have never seen a Christian who took his Christianity literally and really turned the other cheek. But this injunction is one thing when taken literally and something rather different

in its restricted version, which demands the elimination of the sources of violence. No one expects Christians literally to fulfill the commandments of the Gospels; it is expected only that they take seriously the simple and elementary rules of tolerance laid out therein, and refrain from violence. But even this expectation is often considered wildly extravagant. People who like to pride themselves on their realism—as if this word meant anything, or as if any concrete directives could flow from its acceptance—consider the idea of abolishing violence a laughable one. But who is being naive here? Those who think, despite all the evidence of human history, that it is possible to diminish the part violence plays in human relations, that much has already been achieved toward this end, and that more can be peacefully achieved? Or those who imagine that nothing can be accomplished without the use of force, and in particular conversely: that with it everything can be accomplished? No opponent of Christianity can deny that Christianity achieved without the use of force a position in which it could use force against others, and use the name of Jesus as an instrument of torture. It is also true that some forms of practical action based on the principle of applying pressure without violence (for instance, the strategy of Gandhi) have been quite successful. The principle of refraining from violence in international relations is verbally accepted almost universally. Yes, verbally, someone may say; so what? Well, plenty, I would reply. Those values which are verbally accepted and violated in practice are verbally accepted only because of the pressure of universal opinion, which forces agreement. There is no need to despair over hypocrisy; we should, rather, accept that hypocrisy is the testimony to the real social power of those values behind which it hides—the homage that vice pays to virtue, as La Rochefoucauld put it. Until quite recently heads of state did not hesitate openly to announce policies of expansion by war and conquest; but such announcements are now very rare; the idea of a world without violence has been accepted. This being so, the *hope* for a world without violence is not a ludicrous fancy. It is not those who believe that use of force can decline, and who strive to bring about this decline, who are naive, but those who believe that force can resolve everything. This belief is like a kind of infantile fixation. The use of force toward children is unavoidable up to a certain age, but generally decreases with age; sometimes, however, parents extend the use of force for too long and beyond what is necessary. A person brought up in this way generally acquires the conviction that nothing except force can possibly regulate human relations. He builds an infantile view of the world from his own infantile experiences, promoting them to the status of a primitive philosophy of history, which he proudly calls "realistic," "without illusions," etc. In fact, the belief in the omnipotence of force is not only naive but also, in the long run, self-defeating: we know that collectivities which rely only on force and childishly believe in its universal effectiveness are doomed; they cannot survive, precisely because they cannot cope in situations where force is useless. On the other hand, people who are persistent and resolute often achieve their aims without the use of force, but rather by courage joined with intelligence. Renouncing force need not mean resigned passivity or cowed submission: Christ renounced force, but fought relentlessly for his own point of view; and in dying he broke the resistance of those who wielded power and were in a position to use force. The idea of life without force is neither stupid nor utopian. It calls only for courage—a virtue which is most lacking in those who worship force as a universal method, for they are prepared to fight only when they are in a position to use force against those who are weaker, never otherwise.

3. *Man shall not live by bread alone.* Christ quotes this sentence from Deuteronomy, a text he contradicts so often. But he gives it a broader sense: like the lilies and ravens, we should not worry about life and food. Is this, too, a product of pious naiveté? No. For centuries, people have battled for the recognition of values that are not reducible to physical needs and material satisfaction, for the acknowledgment that such values exist, and that they exist independently of all others; and these efforts persist throughout European culture. Such acknowledgment must seem trivial; it does not strike one with its originality. But after the passage of centuries, everything Jesus preached, if it has endured in our culture, comes to seem banal—and it is thanks to him that it has become so. What can be more banal than saying that man does not only clothe himself and eat? And yet the acceptance of this banality sometimes turned out to require a lengthy battle: for instance, a lot of persistent persuasion has gone into arguing that creative works of the human spirit cannot be assessed according to the dubious advantages they might bring to material production. Let us be grateful, then, to the man who reminded us that we do not live by bread alone, while at the same time being aware that the injunction to live like the lilies and ravens cannot be taken literally.

4. *The abolition of the idea of a chosen people.* Jesus opened up God for everyone. Or perhaps he simply completed the opening process begun before him by the Jewish prophets. His God does not forbid his people to

marry the daughters of unbelievers, nor does he require them to destroy other nations; he says that all the righteous are his people; he promises that many will come from east and west, from north and south, to be in God's kingdom with Abraham, Isaac, and Jacob. Jesus' God was filled with love for the world; he so loved it, according to John the apostle, that he gave his only begotten son for its salvation. There was neither Jew nor Greek for him among his people. These, too, are banalities, of course, but they were not banalities when they first entered European culture: they were great causes; problems which, once posed, were irrevocable; values steeped in the blood of those who battled for their recognition. In the realm of theoretical reflection there is no proposal more modest and none that, when taken seriously, has provoked more dramatic conflicts, than the idea that there are no chosen nations, no people beloved above all others by God or by History and entitled thereby to impose their leadership over others in the name of any cause. It was thanks to the teaching of Jesus that this idea—the idea that fundamental human values are the common property of all, and that humanity is one people—became an inalienable part of our spiritual world.

5. *The essential wretchedness of the temporal world.* It does not matter, for these purposes, to what extent the image of the human world as incurably sick is "right." What matters is that this image became an invariable element in the spiritual development of Europe. It is a constantly recurring theme in every variety of philosophical reflection, by no means limited to Christian thought or to thought directly inspired by Christianity. Jesus told people that they were wretched and that they were concealing their wretchedness from themselves. Pascal, when he embraced this belief, made it central to spiritual life. It is true that this idea has sometimes served to check people's desire to improve their temporal lot, to justify a spirit of resignation to their fate, and to extort an acceptance of things as they were; that I was used to quash the protests of the deprived and oppressed when they rebelled against their exploitation; that it was interpreted in a way which made a virtue of discrediting the possibility of any real improvement in the world. It is also true that the chorus of the well fed and well satisfied sometimes clothed itself in the glorious robes of this idea in order to lecture the hungry and deprived about the worthlessness of earthly goods and the pointlessness of worrying about their temporal lot. The history of Christianity so teems with these interpretations that we have almost ceased to notice how revolting they are.

But, despite all this, there is another interpretation; an interpretation that need not entail approval of the privileged and well satisfied. The vileness of this approval was exposed a long time ago and Christianity, as we can see, is slowly renouncing it. The belief in the essential wretchedness of human existence does contain something that can be, and has been, a topic of philosophical reflection, quite independently of the base uses to which it has been put. It is something that has always been an important subject for philosophers; it can be reflected upon regardless of whether or not one believes in an afterlife; and it does not suggest the conclusion that, in view of the structural infirmity of our existence, all efforts to repair what can be repaired are vain and sterile. For one can try to change for the better all that can be changed in the conditions of human existence, one can battle for it relentlessly, while being aware that the absolute is unattainable, and that the essential frailty of human existence is irreparable, because it is a fundamental part of that existence, and arises from human finiteness itself. This topic will not cease to be of interest to philosophers.

RETURNING JESUS TO CULTURE

This is the list—incomplete and selective, but not arbitrarily selective—of the values which, thanks to the teaching of Jesus, found an enduring place in the spiritual substance of Europe and of the world, in a way that was not essentially bound to Christian dogma. But the abstraction of these values, in their non-Christian form, from their personal roots, is a sort of cultural impoverishment. It is connected with the way Jesus has been monopolized by dogmatic Christian communities and with the decline of his presence as a person in other areas of the spiritual world. This poses the risk that all the symptoms of Christianity's decline will, unavoidably, also erode the historical meaning of the existence of Jesus. This is what we want to avoid.

It is true that many of the above-mentioned points could evoke the response "we've heard all this all before"; it is not without justification that we look for similar themes in the religions of Asia. But in Mediterranean culture, the culture of our birth, these values are bound up with the teaching of Jesus and with his name; they are the spiritual fund which he introduced and to which he gave momentum. Hence any attempt to "invalidate Jesus," to eliminate him from our culture on the pretext that we do not believe in the God in whom he believed, is absurd and fruitless. Such attempts are made only by those primitive enough to imagine that crude atheism not only suffices as a view of the world, but can also justify trimming the cultural tradition as one sees fit, according to one's own doctrinal fancies, hacking away an essential part of it and depriving it of its most vital source.

Finally, if—as we uncertainly hope—the Christian world proves capable of real improvement and change, it will draw its reparative strength only from its own source (non-Christian critics can weaken Christianity but they cannot repair it). Consequently, it can maintain its ability for self-repair only by constantly concentrating its attention on that spiritual fund which is bound to the name of Jesus.

Regardless of this hope, however, the person and the teaching of Jesus Christ cannot be invalidated or removed from our culture if that culture is to continue to exist and to create itself. The figure of this man, who for centuries was not just a teacher but the model of the highest human values, cannot fall into oblivion without a fundamental break in the continuity of spiritual life. For he incarnated, in his person, the ability to express one's own truth fully and loudly, to defend it to the end with no evasion, and to resist to the end the pressure of the established reality which rejected him. He taught how we can confront the world and ourselves without resorting to violence. He was a model of that radical authenticity in which, uniquely, every human being can give true life to his own values.

9

How Can One Get from Here to There?

PAUL KINGSWORTH HAS WON awards as a poet and a novelist. He has published influential nonfiction works on international development, the environment, and culture. In 2020, Aris Roussinos called him "England's greatest living writer."[1]

Kingsnorth's personal journey could be described as "a battle against the Machine." During his research for his 2003 book *One No, Many Yeses: A Journey to the Heart of the Global Resistance Movement,*[2] he was tear-gassed on the streets of Genoa, painted anti-World Trade Organization puppets in Johannesburg, met a tribal guerrilla with supernatural powers, took a hot bath in Arizona with a pie-throwing anarchist, and infiltrated the world's biggest gold mine in New Guinea.[3] His later book, *Real England*, lamented how the Machine was homogenizing both countrysides and communities in Britain. In 2009, he co-launched the Dark Mountain Project, a movement of "artists, writers, craftspeople, scientists and other makers, thinkers and doers" trying to face up to "material decline, social and political uncertainty, and ecological collapse." (See Box 1.)

1. Roussinos, "Sailing into Low-Tech Future."
2. The no was to globalization, with diverse and localized yeses the alternatives.
3. From the publisher's blurb.

BOX 1. THE DARK MOUNTAIN PROJECT'S EIGHT
PRINCIPLES OF UNCIVILIZATION[4]

1. We live in a time of social, economic and ecological unravelling. All around us are signs that our whole way of living is already passing into history. We will face this reality honestly and learn how to live with it.

2. We reject the faith which holds that the converging crises of our times can be reduced to a set of "problems" in need of technological or political "solutions."

3. We believe that the roots of these crises lie in the stories we have been telling ourselves. We intend to challenge the stories which underpin our civilization: the myth of progress, the myth of human centrality, and the myth of our separation from "nature." These myths are more dangerous for the fact that we have forgotten they are myths.

4. We will reassert the role of story-telling as more than mere entertainment. It is through stories that we weave reality.

5. Humans are not the point and purpose of the planet. Our art will begin with the attempt to step outside the human bubble. By careful attention, we will reengage with the nonhuman world.

6. We will celebrate writing and art which is grounded in a sense of place and of time. Our literature has been dominated for too long by those who inhabit the cosmopolitan citadels.

7. We will not lose ourselves in the elaboration of theories or ideologies. Our words will be elemental. We write with dirt under our fingernails.

8. The end of the world as we know it is not the end of the world full stop. Together, we will find the hope beyond hope, the paths which lead to the unknown world ahead of us.

4. Kingsnorth, "Eight Principles of Uncivilisation."

Over the next decade, Kingsworth wrote three novels spanning two thousand years of troubled human development.[5]

In the chapter below, Kingsnorth describes key features of his remarkable journey—and how he came to apprehend Christianity as the foil against the Machine.

And for young intellectuals, this aside: in a recent interview, the fifty-two-year-old Kingsnorth said, "My regret is that this didn't happen to me twenty years ago, or thirty! But it's better late than never."[6]

STUDY QUESTIONS

1. As a youth, Kingsnorth and most of his friends dismissed Christianity.

   > The age taught another faith: religion was irrelevant. It was authoritarian, it was superstitious, it was feeble proto-science. It was the theft of our precious free will by authorities who wanted to control us by telling us fairy tales. It repressed women, gay people, atheists, anyone who disobeyed its irrational edicts. It hated science, denied reason, burned witches and heretics by the million. Post-Enlightenment liberal societies had thrown off its shackles, and however hard both species of vicar tried to prevent it, religion was dying a much-needed death at the hands of progress and reason. Et cetera.[7]

   a. What do you think Kingsnorth means by calling these statements about religion "another faith"?

   b. Can you give examples of such teachings in your life?

2. "The rebellion against God" in our modern world "manifested itself in a rebellion against creation, against all nature, human and wild. We would remake Earth, down to the last nanoparticle, to suit our desires, which we now called 'needs.' Our new world would be globalized,

---

5. The last novel in this trilogy, *Alexandria*, is set a thousand years in the future—and it's not a pretty scene.

6. *Big Conversation*, "Rowan Williams & Paul Kingsnorth," 35:08.

7. Kingsnorth, "Cross and Machine," this vol., 154.

uniform, interconnected, digitized, hyperreal, monitored, always on. We were building a machine to replace God."[8]

Appalled, Kingsnorth dove into activism. But eventually, he arrived at the conclusion that

> activism is a staging post on the road to realization. Dig in for long enough and you see that something like climate change or mass extinction is not a "problem" to be "solved" through politics or technology or science, but the manifestation of a deep spiritual malaise. Even an atheist could see that our attempts to play God would end in disaster. Wasn't that a warning that echoed through the myths and stories of every culture on Earth?[9]

    a. How do you understand the idea that climate change and mass extinction are "manifestations of a deep spiritual malaise"?

    b. What do you make of the statement that activism is an "attempt to play God"?

3. "I went searching, then, for the truth," Kingsworth writes. "But where to find it? Elders, saints, and mystics are notable these days for their absence."

> In their place we are offered a pick'n'mix spirituality, on sale in every market stall and pastel-shaded hippy web portal. A dream catcher, a Celtic cross, a book about tantra, a weekend drum workshop, and a pack of tarot cards with cats on them, and hey, presto: you're ready for your personalized "spiritual" journey. On the other side, you will find no exhortation to sacrifice or denial of self, and certainly no battered and bleeding god-man calling you to pick up your cross and follow him. No, you will find instead the perfect manifestation of everything you wanted in the first place: the magnification of your will, not its dissolution. Expressive individualism disguised as epiphany, the reaching prayer of a culture that doesn't know how lost it is.[10]

What are your experiences with "pick'n'mix spirituality"?

8. Kingsnorth, "Cross and Machine," this vol., 155–56. XREF
9. Kingsnorth, "Cross and Machine," this vol., 156. XREF
10. Kingsnorth, "Cross and Machine," this vol., 157. XREF

4. Consider the roles of intellectual arguments in Kingsworth's journey. "In fact, the more I learned, the more Christianity's story about the world and human nature chimed better with my experience than did the increasingly shaky claims of secular materialism. In the end, though, I didn't become a Christian because I could argue myself into it. I became a Christian because I knew, suddenly, that it was true."[11]

   a. Recall times that you concluded that something was true. Describe in your experience the difference between (1) coming to a painstaking conclusion after sifting logic and facts and (2) suddenly just knowing that something is true.

   b. "I can talk for hours," Kingsnorth says of his Christian faith, "but ideas will become idols in the blink of an eye."[12] Have you seen examples of ideas becoming idols? What have been the results?

---

11. Kingsnorth, "Cross and Machine," this vol., 159. XREF
12. Kingsnorth, "Cross and Machine," this vol., 161. XREF

The Cross and the Machine

PAUL KINGSNORTH

"Europeans didn't only disinherit Aztecs and Incas. Continuously, since the sixteenth century, we have been disinheriting ourselves."

—JOHN MORIARTY

"There is no bloodless myth will hold."

—GEOFFREY HILL

We must have been fifteen or sixteen when we discovered the church visitor's book. It was an old church, maybe medieval, and I would pass it with my school friends on our way to the town center. I'm not sure what possessed us to go in; it might have been my idea. I've always loved old churches. For a long time, I would tell myself that I liked the sense of history or the architecture, which was true as far as it went. Like the narrator in Philip Larkin's poem "Church Going," I would venture into any church I found, standing "in awkward reverence . . . wondering what to look for," drawn by some sense that this was "a serious house on serious earth." Obviously, there was no God, but still: the silence of a small church in England had a quality that couldn't be found anywhere else.

This visit was less serious. A fifteen-year-old boy with his schoolmates can't be admitting an interest in rood lofts. I'd like to say it was someone else's idea to write in the visitor's book, where other people had inscribed things like "what a beautiful building" and "I feel a tremendous sense of peace here," but a man should never lie about matters of the soul. It was I who took up the Biro and scrawled, "I WILL DESTROY YOU AND ALL

OF YOUR WORKS! HA HA HA!" then signed it "SATAN." A few days later, we came back and did it again. "DIE, NAZARENE! VICTORY IS MINE!" I think we'd been watching the *Omen* films. We kept going for weeks, wondering when we'd be caught. We never were, but one day we came in to find that all of our entries had been Tipp-Exed out and the pen removed. The fun was over. We went to the video shop instead.

More than thirty years later, in the early spring of 2020, I was reading the autobiography of the Irish philosopher John Moriarty and following the news about some new virus that was apparently spreading in China. Moriarty's book is called *Nostos*—homecoming—and like all his work, it is impossible to summarize because it is less a narrative than a myth. One of its threads, though, is how Moriarty gave up on the simple, unconvincing Christianity of his Irish rural youth and left for Canada to become an academic, only to become equally disillusioned with the empty-can rationalism that characterizes postmodern intellectual culture. Something was missing. Was it Ireland? Moriarty threw in his academic career and moved back to the mountains of Connacht. He had lost faith in science, in the mind alone of itself, in an age that had disinherited its people. But even at home, some part of the jigsaw was missing.

Seeking it, whatever it was, Moriarty crashed into a devastating personal crisis. One day, walking in the mountains, he suddenly had a mystical vision that broke his world apart. "In an instant," he wrote, "I was ruined." He seemed to see into a great abyss in which all of his stories were dust: "I had been let through not to a heaven but to a void that was starless and fatherless." For years, he wrote, he had been engaged in "a genuine search for the truth, not merely a speakable truth, but a truth I would surrender to." Now he realized, with a terrible inevitability, that there was only one story that could hold what he had seen, only "one prayer that was big enough." He had, he wrote, been "shattered into seeing." Whether he liked it or not, he had become a Christian.

A truth I would surrender to. I put the book down. I didn't know quite why, but Moriarty's story had shaken me. I realized that I had been searching for years for a truth like that. "How strange!" he had written. "Christianity making sense to me!" Somehow, the way he was telling the story—interweaving the Gospels with the book of Job, the Mahabharata, the Pali Canon of the Buddha, the folk tales of Ireland, the poems of Wallace Stevens—was making sense to me too. What was going on?

"The story of Christianity," wrote Moriarty, "is the story of humanity's rebellion against God." I had never thought of that ancient, tired religion in this way before, never had reason to, but as I did now I could feel something happening—some inner shift, some coming together of previously scattered parts designed to fit, though I had never known it, into a quiet, unbreakable whole.

A truth I would surrender to. What was this abyss inside me, this space that had been empty for years, that I had tried to fill with everything from sex to fame to politics to *kenshō*, and why was something chiming in it now like a distant Angelus across the western sea?

> *For the thing which I greatly feared is come upon me,*
> *And that which I was afraid of is come unto me.*

Something was happening to me, and I didn't like it at all.

Urban England in the eighties was not, shall we say, a spiritually rich environment. My family never set foot in a church when I was growing up, which suited me fine. The nearest I came to serious religion was probably through my best friend, who was from a Pakistani family. He'd been on the hajj to Mecca and fasted for Ramadan and did all the other things that Muslims did, which I knew very little about. This was before Islam became a political lightning rod and everyone felt they had to develop strong opinions about it. All I knew was that my friend thought religion was real, which seemed quaint and very un-English. We in the modern world had long grown out of superstition.

Still, at least my friend's religion seemed to pulse with some sort of living energy. The same could not be said of the Christianity which, when I was a child, was still at least nominally the national faith. I grew up singing hymns, listening to parables recited by teachers at morning assembly, and performing in Christmas nativity plays with a tea towel tied around my head. I knew the Lord's Prayer by heart. Whether I liked it or not, I was taught as a child the outline of the Christian story—the story that had shaped my nation for more than a thousand years. I didn't realize that my nation was surviving on spiritual credit, and that it was coming close to running out.

Back then, there were two distinct flavors of Christianity, both of which I tried to avoid. One was the fusty old Church of England variety. You would see this if you had to go to a wedding or a funeral, or when a vicar was invited to give a sermon at school. The vicar would be a slightly

Victorian figure, an older man almost dainty in his manners, trying his best to speak in a dying tongue to a generation of kids more interested in their ZX Spectrums. The Victorian vicar would hand out morality lessons from a man who had lived two thousand years ago and whose core imagery might as well have been from Mars: wine presses, fishing boats, vineyards, masters and servants, virgins. The basic pitch seemed best summed up by Douglas Adams in The *Hitchhiker's Guide to the Galaxy*, which I'd rather have been reading than listening to a vicar: "One man had been nailed to a tree for saying how great it would be to be nice to people for a change."

The second flavor was the trendy vicar. Unlike his predecessor, the trendy vicar was plugged into the spirit of the age. He knew that instead of bicycling to Holy Communion through the morning mist, we were watching *The Young Ones* and playing Manic Miner, and he was on our side. The trendy vicar had a clipped beard and wore jeans and sang folk songs about how Jesus was our friend, and gave awkward, vernacular sermons in which biblical stories were interspersed with references to *EastEnders* or *Dallas* or Michael Jackson songs. Despite his good intentions, the trendy vicar was much worse than the stuffy vicar. At least the Victorian sermons were in some way otherworldly, as religion should be. If it was pop culture we wanted, and we did, we were better off sticking with the real thing, which was to say the thing without any Jesus in it.

So, I had no reason to take any notice of religion in general or Christianity in particular. My Muslim friend had a faith that was passed to him by his family and was clearly a central part of their worldview. Nothing similar was offered to me, and even if it were, it would have been undercut by the wider cultural narrative. The school may have had mandatory religious education classes, but the age taught another faith: religion was irrelevant. It was authoritarian, it was superstitious, it was feeble proto-science. It was the theft of our precious free will by authorities who wanted to control us by telling us fairy tales. It repressed women, gay people, atheists, anyone who disobeyed its irrational edicts. It hated science, denied reason, burned witches and heretics by the million. Post-Enlightenment liberal societies had thrown off its shackles, and however hard both species of vicar tried to prevent it, religion was dying a much-needed death at the hands of progress and reason.

Et cetera.

Still, there was enough truth in this story to fuel the intellectual anger of the Dawkins-esque teenage atheist that I later became. People had walked away from the church by choice, after all, and not just because they all wanted to have premarital sex. The message seemed irrelevant. Across Europe, the exodus was happening. Corrupted, tired, suddenly powerless, Christianity was dying in the West. And why not? I hadn't seen anything relevant in it. Where was the mystery? Where was the promised connection with God? Who was this God anyway? A man in the sky with a book of rules? It was long past time to move on.

I didn't know back then that the Christian story is the story of our rebellion against God. I didn't know that by taking part in that rebellion I had become part of the story, whether I liked it or not. I didn't know, either, why Christians see pride as the greatest sin. I only knew that I could argue a good case for the injustice of the world made by this "God," and the silliness of miracles, resurrections, and virgin births. I knew I was cleverer than all the people who believed this sort of rubbish, and I was happy to tell them so.

I kept visiting empty churches. I just didn't tell anyone.

Up on the mountains of England and Wales, I had my own visions. Walking and camping on the hills for weeks with my dad, I felt something settle within me that was more real than any theology. I might have been a teenage atheist, but my atheism amounted mainly to arguing with Christians. The religions of the book were obviously nonsense, but I knew there was something going on that humans couldn't grasp. Trudging across moors, camping by mountain lakes as the June sun set, I could feel some deep, old power rolling through it all, welding it together, flowing from the land into me and back again. With Wordsworth, I was dragged under by "A motion and a spirit, that impels / All thinking things, all objects of all thought / And rolls through all things." Nothing humans could build could come close to the intense wonder and mystery of the natural world; I still believe that to be self-evidently true. This was my religion. Animism, pantheism, call it what you will: this was my pagan grace.

Years of environmental activism followed. Working for NGOs, writing for magazines, chaining myself to things, marching, occupying: whatever you did, you had to do something, for the state of the Earth was dire. Nobody with eyes to see can deny what humanity has done to the living tissue of the planet, though plenty still try. There were big, systemic reasons for it, I discovered: capitalism, industrialism, maybe civilization itself. Whatever had got us here, it was clear where we were going: into a world in which industrial humanity has ravaged much of the wild earth, tamed the rest, and shaped all nature to its ends. The rebellion against God manifested itself in a rebellion against creation, against all nature, human and wild. We would remake Earth, down to the last nanoparticle, to suit our desires, which we now called "needs." Our new world would be globalized, uniform, interconnected, digitized, hyperreal, monitored, always on. We were building a machine to replace God.

Activism is a staging post on the road to realization. Dig in for long enough and you see that something like climate change or mass extinction is not a "problem" to be "solved" through politics or technology or science, but the manifestation of a deep spiritual malaise. Even an atheist could see that our attempts to play God would end in disaster. Wasn't that a warning that echoed through the myths and stories of every culture on Earth?

Early Green thinkers, people like Leopold Kohr or E. F. Schumacher, who were themselves inspired by the likes of Gandhi and Tolstoy, had taught us that the ecological crisis was above all a crisis of limits, or lack of them. Modern economies thrive by encouraging ever-increasing consumption of harmful junk, and our hyper-liberal culture encourages us to satiate any and all of our appetites in our pursuit of happiness. If that pursuit turns out to make us unhappy instead—well, that's probably just because some limits remain un-busted.

Following the rabbit hole down, I realized that a crisis of limits is a crisis of culture, and a crisis of culture is a crisis of spirit. Every living culture in history, from the smallest tribe to the largest civilization, has been built around a spiritual core: a central claim about the relationship between human culture, nonhuman nature, and divinity. Every culture that lasts, I suspect, understands that living within limits—limits set by natural law, by cultural tradition, by ecological boundaries—is a cultural necessity and a spiritual imperative. There seems to be only one culture in history that has held none of this to be true, and it happens to be the one we're living in.

Now I started to dimly see something I ought to have seen years before: that the great spiritual pathways, the teachings of the saints and gurus and mystics, and the vessels built to hold them—vessels we call "religions"— might have been there for a reason. They might even have been telling us something urgent about human nature, and what happens when our reach exceeds our grasp. G. K. Chesterton once declared, contra Marx, that it was irreligion that was the opium of the people. "Wherever the people do not believe in something beyond the world," he explained, "they will worship the world. But above all, they will worship the strongest thing in the world." Here we were.

I went searching, then, for the truth. But where to find it? Elders, saints, and mystics are notable these days for their absence. In their place we are offered a pick'n'mix spirituality, on sale in every market stall and pastel-shaded hippy web portal. A dream catcher, a Celtic cross, a book about tantra, a weekend drum workshop, and a pack of tarot cards with cats on them, and hey, presto: you're ready for your personalized "spiritual" journey. On the other side, you will find no exhortation to sacrifice or denial of self, and certainly no battered and bleeding god-man calling you to pick up your cross and follow him. No, you will find instead the perfect manifestation of everything you wanted in the first place: the magnification of your will, not its dissolution. Expressive individualism disguised as epiphany, the reaching prayer of a culture that doesn't know how lost it is.

I wanted something more serious, something with structure, rules, a tradition. It didn't even occur to me to go and ask the vicars. I knew that Christianity, with its instructions to man to "dominate and subdue" the Earth, was part of the problem. And so, I looked east. On my fortieth birthday I treated myself to a weeklong Zen retreat in the Welsh mountains. The effect of seven days of disciplined meditation in a farmhouse with no electricity was astonishing. Something in me flipped open. For the next five or six years, I practiced *Zazen* and studied the teachings of the Buddha. It is clear enough why Buddhism is taking off in the West as Christianity declines: its metaphysical claims seem convincing, its practices, when taught properly, yield results, and as a tradition it is even older than Christianity. It is, in short, a serious spiritual path, but with none of the cultural baggage of the church.

And yet. As the years went on, Zen was not enough. It was full of compassion, but it lacked love. It lacked something else too, and it took me a long time to admit to myself what it was: I wanted to worship. My teenage atheist self would have been horrified. Something was happening to me, slowly, steadily, that I didn't understand but could clearly sense. I felt like I was being filed gently into a new shape.

Something was calling me. But what?

Obviously, it wasn't Christ. I had read the New Testament a few times, and I mostly liked what I saw. Who couldn't admire this man or see that, at root, he was teaching the truth? Still, he obviously didn't die and return to life, this being impossible, and without that, the faith built around him was nonsense. I was a pagan, anyway. I found God in nature, so I needed a nature religion.

This was how I ended up a priest of the witch gods.

The short version of the story is that I joined my local Wiccan coven. Wicca is a relatively new occult tradition, founded in the 1950s by the eccentric Englishman Gerald Gardner, who claimed he had discovered the ancient remnant of a pre-Christian goddess cult. He was fibbing, but the practice he sewed together out of older, disparate parts is strangely cohesive, complete with secret initiatory rituals, a law book that can be copied only by hand by initiates, magical teachings, spell work, protective circles, and, at the heart of it all, the worship of two deities: the great goddess and the horned god. All initiated Wiccans are priests or priestesses of these gods; there are no laity. My coven used to do its rituals in the woods under the full moon. It was fun, and it made things happen. I discovered that magic is real. It works. Who it works for is another question.

At last I was home, where I belonged: in the woods, worshipping a nature goddess under the stars. I even got to wear a cloak. Everything seemed to have fallen into place. Until I started having dreams.

I had known, I suppose, that the abyss was still there inside me—that what I was doing in the woods, though affecting, was at some level still play-acting. Then, one night, I dreamed of Jesus. The dream was vivid, and when I woke up I wrote down what I had heard him say, and I drew what he had looked like. The crux of the matter was that he was to be the next step on my spiritual path. I didn't believe that or want it to be true. But the image and the message reminded me of something strange that had happened a few months before. My wife and I were out to dinner, celebrating our wedding anniversary, when suddenly she said to me, "You're going to become a Christian." When I asked her what on earth she was talking about, she said she didn't know; she had just had a feeling and needed to tell me. My wife has a preternatural sensitivity that she always denies, and it wasn't the first time she had done something like this. It shook me. A Christian? Me? What could be weirder?

After the dream, it began to make sense. Suddenly, I started meeting Christians everywhere. They were coming out of the woodwork: strangers emailing me out of the blue, priests coming to me for help with their writing. I found myself having conversations with friends I'd never known were Christian, who suddenly seemed to want to talk about it. An African man contacted me on Facebook to tell me he had had a dream in which God had told him to convert me. "If you want to know God," he told me, "you need to read the book He wrote. You know it already: It's called nature."

It kept happening, for months. Christ to the left of me, Christ to the right. It was unnerving. I turned away again and again, but every time I looked back, he was still there. I began to feel I was being . . . hunted? I wanted it to stop; at least, I thought I did. I had no interest in Christianity. I was a witch! A Zen witch, in fact, which I thought sounded pretty damned edgy. But I knew who was after me, and I knew it wasn't over.

One evening, I was sitting in the kitchen of the house in which our coven had its temple. We were about to go in and conduct an important ritual. As we got up to leave, I felt violently ill. I was dizzy, I was sick, I was lightheaded. Everyone noticed and fussed over me as I sat down, my face pale. I had an overpowering feeling that I should not go into the temple. I felt I was being physically prevented from doing it. Someone had staged an intervention.

After that, there was no escape. Like C. S. Lewis, I could not ignore "the steady, unrelenting approach of Him whom I so earnestly desired not to meet." How much later was it that I was finally pinned down? I don't remember. I was at a concert at my son's music school. We were in a hotel function room, full of children ready to play their instruments and proud parents ready to film them doing it. I was just walking to my chair when I was overcome entirely. Suddenly, I could see how everyone in the room was connected to everyone else, and I could see what was going on inside them and inside myself. I was overcome with a huge and inexplicable love, a great wave of empathy, for everyone and everything. It kept coming and coming until I had to stagger out of the room and sit down in the corridor outside. Everything was unchanged, and everything was new, and I knew what had happened and who had done it, and I knew that it was too late. I had just become a Christian.

None of this is rationally explicable, and there is no point in arguing with me about it. There is no point in my arguing with myself about it: I gave up after a while. This is not to say that my faith is irrational. In fact, the more I learned, the more Christianity's story about the world and human nature chimed better with my experience than did the increasingly shaky claims of secular materialism. In the end, though, I didn't become a Christian because I could argue myself into it. I became a Christian because I knew, suddenly, that it was true. The Angelus that was chiming in the abyss is silent now, for the abyss is gone. Someone else inhabits me.

I am not a joiner, but I accepted, eventually, that I would need a church. I went looking, and I found one, as usual, in the last place I expected. This January, on the feast of Theophany, I was baptized in the freezing waters of the River Shannon, on a day of frost and sun, into the Romanian Orthodox Church. In Orthodoxy I had found the answers I had sought, in the one place I never thought to look. I found a Christianity that had retained its ancient heart—a faith with living saints and a central ritual of deep and inexplicable power. I found a faith that, unlike the one I had seen as a boy, was not a dusty moral template but a mystical path, an ancient and rooted thing, pointing to a world in which the divine is not absent but everywhere present, moving in the mountains and the waters. The story I had heard a thousand times turned out to be a story I had never heard at all.

Out in the world, the rebellion against God has become a rebellion against everything: roots, culture, community, families, biology itself. Machine progress—the triumph of the Nietzschean will—dissolves the glue that once held us. Fires are set around the supporting pillars of the culture by those charged with guarding it, urged on by an ascendant faction determined to erase the past, abuse their ancestors, and dynamite their cultural inheritance, the better to build their earthly paradise on *terra nullius*. Massing against them are the new Defenders of the West, some calling for a return to the atomized liberalism that got us here in the first place, others defending a remnant Christendom that seems to have precious little to do with Christ and forgets Christopher Lasch's warning that "God, not culture, is the only appropriate object of unconditional reverence and wonder." Two profane visions going head-to-head, when what we are surely crying out for is the only thing that can heal us: a return to the sacred center around which any real culture is built.

Up on the mountain like Moriarty, in the Maumturk ranges in the autumn rain, I had my own vision, terrible and joyful and impossible. I saw that if we were to follow the teachings we were given at such great cost—the radical humility, the blessings upon the meek, the love of neighbor and enemy, the woe unto those who are rich, the last who will be first—above all, if we were to stumble toward the Creator with love and awe, then creation itself would not now be groaning under our weight. I saw that the teachings of Christ were the most radical in history, and that no empire could be built by those who truly lived them. I saw that we had arrived here because we do not live them; because, as Auden had it:

> We would rather be ruined than changed.
> We would rather die in our dread
> Than climb the cross of the moment
> And let our illusions die.

It turns out that both the stuffy vicars and the trendy vicars were onto something: the Cross holds the key to everything. The sacrifice is all the teaching. I am a new and green pupil. I can talk for hours, but ideas will become idols in the blink of an eye. I have to pick up my cross and start walking.

How can I feel I have arrived home in something that is in many ways so foreign to me? And yet beneath the surface it is not foreign at all, but a reversion to the sacred order of things. I sit in a monastery chapel before dawn. There is snow on the ground outside. The priest murmurs the liturgy by the light of the *lampadas*, the dark silhouettes of two nuns chant the antiphon. There is incense in the air. The icons glow in the half light. This could be a thousand years in the past or the future, for in here, there is no time. Home is beyond time, I think now. I can't explain any of it, and it is best that I do not try.

I grew up believing what all modern people are taught: that freedom meant lack of constraint. Orthodoxy taught me that this freedom was no freedom at all, but enslavement to the passions: a neat description of the first thirty years of my life. True freedom, it turns out, is to give up your will and follow God's. To deny yourself. To let it come. I am terrible at this, but at least now I understand the path.

In the Kingdom of Man, the seas are ribboned with plastic, the forests are burning, the cities bulge with billionaires and tented camps, and still we kneel before the idol of the great god Economy as it grows and grows like a cancer cell. And what if this ancient faith is not an obstacle after all, but a way through? As we see the consequences of eating the forbidden fruit, of choosing power over humility, separation over communion, the stakes become clearer each day. Surrender or rebellion; sacrifice or conquest; death of the self or triumph of the will; the Cross or the machine. We have always been offered the same choice. The gate is strait and the way is narrow and maybe we will always fail to walk it. But is there any other road that leads home?

Bibliography

Adams, Douglas. *The Hitchhiker's Guide to the Galaxy*. New York: Harmony, 1979.

Agassi, Joseph. "Genius in Science." *Philosophy of the Social Sciences* 5 (1975) 145–61.

Allen, Summer. *The Science of Awe*. Berkeley: Greater Good Science Center, University of California, 2018. https://www.templeton.org/wp-content/uploads/2018/08/White-Paper_Awe_FINAL.pdf.

Allison, Scott T., and George R. Goethals. *Heroes: Who They Are and What They Do*. Oxford: Oxford University Press, 2011.

———. *Heroic Leadership: An Influence Taxonomy of 100 Exceptional Individuals*. Leadership: Research and Practice. London: Routledge, 2013.

Altizer, Thomas J. J. "The Protestant Jesus: Milton and Blake." In *The Contemporary Jesus*, 115–37. Albany: SUNY Press, 1997.

Appleyard, Bryan. *Understanding the Present: Science and the Soul of Modern Man*. New York: Doubleday, 1993.

Begley, Louis. *Mistler's Exit: A Novel*. New York: Knopf, 1998.

Bérard, Alexandre. *Les Vaudois*. Lyon: Storck, 1892.

Big Conversation, The. "Rowan Williams & Paul Kingsnorth: Conversion, Culture, and the Cross." YouTube, June 3, 2022. From *The Big Conversation*, episode 2, season 4. https://youtu.be/iCxznkRKa1w?si=wNGEY0SpuRNVRpu6.

Billington, James H. "Leszek Kolakowski: Scholar and Activist; The Long Career of the Kluge Prize Winner." *Library of Congress Information Bulletin* 62 (2003). https://www.loc.gov/loc/lcib/0312/kluge2.html.

Bornstein, David. *How to Change the World: Social Entrepreneurs and the Power of New Ideas*. Oxford: Oxford University Press, 2004.

Bradley, A. C. *Shakespearean Tragedy: Lectures on Hamlet, Othello, King Lear, Macbeth*. London: Macmillan, 1904.

Brunner, Emil. *Our Faith*. Translated by John W. Rilling. New York: Scribner's Sons. 1962. First published 1936.

Campbell, Joseph. *The Hero with a Thousand Faces*. 3rd ed. *The Collected Works of Joseph Campbell*. Bollingen Series 17. Novato, California: New World Library, 2008. First published 1949.

———. "The Hero with a Thousand Faces." Interview with Bill Moyers. YouTube, June 18, 2021. https://youtu.be/Byli-Y8KonY.

Camus, Albert. *The Fall*. Translated by Justin O'Brien. New York: Vintage, 1956.

Carey, John, ed. *The Faber Book of Science*. London: Faber and Faber, 1995.

Colby, Anne, and William Damon. *Some Do Care: Contemporary Lives of Moral Commitment.* New York: Free, 1992.

Crossan, John Dominic. *The Historical Jesus: The Life of a Mediterranean Jewish Peasant.* New York: HarperCollins, 1992.

Curtius, Ernst Robert. *European Literature and the Latin Middle Ages.* Translated by Willard R. Trask. Bollingen Series 36. Princeton, NJ: Princeton University Press, 1953. First published 1948.

Dillard, Annie. *An American Childhood.* New York: Harper & Row, 1987.

———. *Holy the Firm.* New York: Harper and Row, 1977.

———. *Pilgrim at Tinker Creek.* New York: Harper & Row, 1974.

———. "This Is the Life." *The Abundance: Narrative Essays Old and New,* 117–22. New York: HarperCollins, 2016.

Ehrman, Bart D. *Jesus, Interrupted: Revealing the Hidden Contradictions in the Bible (and Why We Don't Know about Them).* New York: HarperOne, 2010.

EPSRC. "Memorandum Submitted by the Engineering and Physical Sciences Research Council." Parliament of the United Kingdom, Feb. 25, 1998. https://publications. parliament.uk/pa/cm199798/cmselect/cmsctech/626-i/626i02.htm.

Escrivá, Josemaría. *The Way.* New York: Doubleday, 1982. First published 1939.

Ganzevoort, Reinder Ruard. "Crisis Experiences and the Development of Belief and Unbelief." In *Belief and Unbelief: Psychological Perspectives,* edited by Jozef Corveleyn and Dirk Hutsebaut, 21–36. Amsterdam: Rodopi BV, 1994.

Gibson, Mel, dir. *The Passion of the Christ.* Los Angeles: Newmarket, 2004.

Gopnik, Adam. *The Real Work: On the Mystery of Mastery.* New York: Liveright, 2023.

———. "What Did Jesus Do?" *New Yorker,* May 17, 2010. https://www.newyorker.com/ magazine/2010/05/24/what-did-jesus-do.

Gribbin, John, and Martin Rees. *Cosmic Coincidences.* New York: Bantam, 1989.

Hearn, Richard Jock. *The Soldier and the Monk.* Ann Arbor: University Microfilms International, 1984.

Hesse, Hermann. *The Glass Bead Game [Magister ludi].* Translated by Richard Winston and Clara Winston. New York: Holt, Rinehart and Winston, 1969. First published 1943.

Hook, Sidney. *The Hero in History: A Study in Limitation and Possibility.* Boston: Beacon, 1955. First published 1943.

Hyde, Lewis. *The Gift: Creativity and the Artist in the Modern World.* New York: Vintage, 2007. First published 1983.

"Imitation of Christ." New Advent, n.d. Edited by Kevin Knight. From *The Catholic Encyclopedia,* vol. 7. New York: Appleton, 1910. http://www.newadvent.org/cath en/07674c.htm.

Jacobovici, Simcha, dir. *The Lost Tomb of Jesus.* Aired Mar. 4, 2007, on Discovery.

James, William. "Is Life Worth Living?" In *The Will to Believe: And Other Essays in Popular Philosophy.* London: Longman, 1912. First published 1895. https://www.gutenberg. org/files/26659/26659-h/26659-h.htm#P22.

———. *The Varieties of Religious Experience: A Study in Human Nature.* New York: Longman, Green, 1917. First published 1902. https://www.gutenberg.org/files/ 621/621-h/621-h.html.

Jenkins, John Philip. *Jesus Wars: How Four Patriarchs, Three Queens, and Two Emperors Decided What Christians Would Believe for the Next 1,500 Years.* New York: Harper One, 2010.

Jenkins, Thomas E. *The Character of God: Recovering the Lost Literary Power of American Protestantism.* New York: Oxford University Press, 1997.

Johnson, Paul. *Heroes: From Alexander the Great and Julius Caesar to Churchill and De Gaulle.* New York: Harper, 2007.

———. *Jesus: A Biography, from a Believer.* New York: Penguin, 2011.

Jones, E. Stanley. *The Way.* Nashville: Abingdon-Cokesbury, 1946.

Juliani, Michael. "Lisa Wells: Tapering of Extremes." *Guernica*, May 22, 2018. https://www.guernicamag.com/lisa-wells-tapering-of-extremes/.

Jung, Carl G. *The Development of Personality.* Translated by Gerhard Adler and R. F. C. Hull. Vol. 17 of *The Collected Works of C. G. Jung.* Princeton, NJ: Princeton University Press, 1955. First published 1910.

Kempis, Thomas à. *The Imitation of Christ.* Translated by Leo Sherley-Price. London: Penguin, 1952. First published 1441.

Kermode, Frank. *The Genesis of Secrecy: On the Interpretation of Narrative.* Cambridge, MA: Harvard University Press, 1979.

Kierkegaard, Søren. *Fear and Trembling.* Translated by Walter Lowrie. New York: Anchor, 1954. First published 1843.

Kingsnorth, Paul. *Alexandria: A Novel.* London: Faber & Faber, 2020.

———. "Eight Principles of Uncivilisation." Resilience, May 15, 2010. From the Dark Mountain Project. https://www.resilience.org/stories/2010-05-15/eight-principles-uncivilisation/.

———. *One No, Many Yeses: A Journey to the Heart of the Global Resistance Movement.* London: Free, 2003.

———. *Real England: The Battle against the Bland.* London: Portobello, 2008.

Kinsella, Elaine Louise, et al. "Zeroing In on Heroes: A Prototype Analysis of Hero Features." *Journal of Personality and Social Psychology* 108 (2015) 114–27.

Klitgaard, Robert. "From Insight to Ideology." *Theoria* 83/84 (1994) 167–77.

———. "Hermits, Addicts, and Heroes." *International Journal of Religion and Spirituality in Society* 10 (2020) 29–40.

———. *Prevail: How to Face Upheavals and Make Big Choices with the Help of Heroes.* Eugene: Wipf & Stock, 2022.

Kołakowski, Leszek. "Jesus Christ—Prophet and Reformer." In *Is God Happy? Selected Essays*, translated by Agnieszka Kołakowska, 143–60. New York: Basic, 2013. First published 1956.

———. *Świadomość religijna i więź kościelna. Studia nad chrześcijaństwem bezwyznaniowym XVII wieku.* Warsaw: Naukowe PWN, 1997. First published 1965.

Langer, Suzanne K. *Philosophy in a New Key: A Study in the Symbolism of Reason, Rite, and Art.* 3rd ed. Cambridge, MA: Harvard University Press, 1957.

Lewis, C. S. *The Last Battle.* London: Bodley Head, 1956.

Lowell, James Russell. "The Present Crisis." Poets, 1845. https://poets.org/poem/present-crisis.

Macaulay, Thomas Babington. *Macaulay: Poetry and Prose.* Edited by G. M. Young. Cambridge, MA: Harvard University Press, 1967. First published 1927.

MacCulloch, Diarmaid. *Christianity: The First Three Thousand Years.* New York: Viking, 2010.

Maslow, Abraham H. "Cognition of Being in the Peak Experience." *Journal of General Psychology* 95 (1959) 43–66.

———. *The Farther Reaches of Human Nature.* New York: Viking, 1971.

———. *Toward a Psychology of Being.* New York: Van Nostrand, 1962.

Matthews, Steve. "Chronic Automaticity in Addiction: Why Extreme Addiction Is a Disorder." *Neuroethics* 10 (2017) 199–209.

Mawson, T. J. *God and the Meanings of Life: What God Could and Couldn't Do to Make Our Lives More Meaningful.* London: Bloomsbury, 2016.

Mead, Margaret, and Paul Byers. *The Small Conference: An Innovation in Communication.* Paris: Mouton & Co., 1968.

Miles, Jack. "Crucifixion and the Conscience of the West." In *Christ: A Crisis in the Life of God*, 3–12. New York: Knopf, 2001.

———. *God: A Biography.* New York: Knopf, 1995.

———, ed. *The Norton Anthology of World Religions.* 2 vols. New York: Norton, 2014.

———. "War, Peace, and a Crisis in the Life of God." Random House, 2002. https://www.randomhouse.com/knopf/authors/miles/essay.html#essay.

Miller, Lisa. "Why Harvard Students Should Study More Religion." *Newsweek*, Feb. 10, 2010; updated Mar. 13, 2010. https://www.newsweek.com/why-harvard-students-should-study-more-religion-75231.

Moltmann, Jürgen. *The Crucified God: The Cross of Christ as the Foundation and Criticism of Christian Theology.* Minneapolis: Fortress, 1993. First published 1972.

Moorhouse, Geoffrey. *Beyond All Reason: Monastic Life in the Twentieth Century.* London: Weidenfeld & Nicolson, 1969.

Moriarty, John. *Nostos: An Autobiography.* Dublin: Liliput, 2011.

Nagy, Gregory. *The Ancient Greek Hero in 24 Hours.* Cambridge, MA: Harvard University Press, 2013.

———. "The Epic Hero." Center for Hellenic Studies, 2005. 2nd ed. (online version). http://nrs.harvard.edu/urn-3:hlnc.essay:Nagy.The_Epic_Hero.2005.

Nakamura, Jeanne, and Mihaly Csikszentmihalyi. "The Construction of Meaning through Vital Engagement." In *Flourishing: Positive Psychology and the Life Well-Lived*, edited by Corey L. M. Keyes and Jonathan Haidt, 83–104. Washington, DC: American Psychological Association, 2003.

Nietzsche, Friedrich. *Der Fall Wagner. Götzen-Dämmerung. Der Antichrist. Ecce Homo. Dionysos-Dithyramben. Nietzsche contra Wagner.* Edited by Giorgio Colli and Mazzino Montinari. Sämtliche Werke 6. Munich: Deutscher Taschenbuch, 1988.

———. *The Portable Nietzsche.* Edited and translated by Walter Kaufmann. New York: Penguin, 1959.

———. *Thus Spake Zarathustra: A Book for All and None.* Translated by Thomas Common. New York: Macmillan, 1911. First published 1883.

Otto, Rudolph. *The Idea of the Holy: An Inquiry into the Non-rational Factor in the Idea of the Divine and Its Relation to the Rational.* Translated by John W. Harvey. Oxford: Oxford University Press, 1958. First published 1917.

Poon, Wilson, and Tom McLeish. "Real Presences: Two Scientists' Response to George Steiner." *Theology* 102 (1999) 169–77.

Pullman, Philip. *The Good Man Jesus and the Scoundrel Christ.* Edinburgh: Canongate, 2011.

Roussinos, Ari. "Sailing into a Low-Tech Future." *UnHerd*, Aug. 21, 2020. https://unherd.com/newsroom/sailing-into-a-low-tech-future/.

Schopenhauer, Arthur. *The World as Will and Idea.* Translated by Jill Berman. London: Everyman, 1995. First published 1819.

Seligman, Martin E. P. *Authentic Happiness.* New York: Free, 2002.

Shearman, John K. G. *Only Connect: Art and the Spectator in the Italian Renaissance.* A. W. Mellon Lectures in the Fine Arts. Bollingen Series. Princeton, NJ: Princeton University Press, 1988.

Steinbeck, John. *The Log from the Sea of Cortez.* New York: Viking, 1951.

Steiner, George. *A Festival Overture: The University Festival Lecture.* Edinburgh: University of Edinburgh, 1996.

———. *Language and Silence.* London: Faber and Faber, 1985.

———. *Real Presences.* London: Faber and Faber, 1989.

Stip, Emmanuel, et al. "Internet Addiction, Hikikomori Syndrome, and the Prodromal Phase of Psychosis." *Frontiers in Psychiatry* 7 (2016) 2–8.

Tabor, James. *The Jesus Dynasty: The Hidden History of Jesus, His Royal Family, and the Birth of Christianity.* New York: Simon and Schuster, 2006.

Thomson, James. *The City of Dreadful Night and Other Poems.* London: Reeves and Turner, 1880. First published 1874.

Thorp, Charley Linden. "Mahayana Buddhism." Brewminate, Mar. 15, 2017. https://brewminate.com/mahayana-buddhism/.

Tippett, Krista. "Adam Gopnik: Practicing Doubt, Redrawing Faith." *On Being,* Nov. 5, 2015; last updated Dec. 7, 2017. https://onbeing.org/programs/adam-gopnik-practicing-doubt-redrawing-faith-dec2017/.

———. "Krista Tippett in Conversation with Roberto Mangabeira Unger." Otter, Dec. 26, 2021. Recorded 2014. https://otter.ai/u/T81qWsV3UiPCqa3fLNwtr9VGRqo.

Unger, Roberto Mangabeira. "Beyond the Small Life: A Letter to Young People." YouTube, 2002. https://youtu.be/pdb-GTjggTg?si=8VHZPwRJHsTQTomC.

———. *The Religion of the Future.* Cambridge, MA: Harvard University Press, 2014.

———. *The Self Awakened: Pragmatism Unbound.* Cambridge, MA: Harvard University Press, 2007.

———. "The Universal Grid of Philosophy." In *The Self Awakened: Pragmatism Unbound,* 243–56. Cambridge, MA: Harvard University Press, 2007. https://www.robertounger.com/_files/ugd/5e60f9_2d1588cc3a824d5fb3b801f83cbf3137.pdf.

———. *The World and Us.* London: Verso, 2024.

Updike, John. "Perfection Wasted." In *Collected Poems: 1953–1993,* 353. New York: Knopf, 1995.

Verhoeven, Paul. *Jesus of Nazareth.* New York: Seven Stories, 2010.

Waring, George E. *Tyrol and the Skirt of the Alps.* New York: Harper, 1880.

Weber, Max. "Politics as a Vocation." In *From Max Weber: Essays in Sociology,* edited and translated by H. H. Gerth and C. Wright Mills, 77–128. Oxford: Oxford University Press, 1946. First published 1919.

Weinberg, Steven. *Dreams of a Final Theory: The Scientist's Search for the Ultimate Laws of Nature.* New York: Knopf, 1992.

Wells, Lisa. *Believers: Making a Life at the End of the World.* New York: Farrar, Straus and Giroux, 2021.

Wheelis, Allen. *The Listener: A Psychoanalyst Examines His Life.* New York: Norton, 1999.

White, L. Michael. *Scripting Jesus: The Gospels in Rewrite.* New York: HarperOne, 2010.

Worthington, Everett L., and Scott T. Allison. *Heroic Humility: What the Science of Humility Can Say to People Raised on Self-Focus.* Washington, DC: American Psychological Association, 2018.

Zimbardo, Philip G. "What Makes a Hero?" *Greater Good Magazine,* Jan. 18, 2011. https://greatergood.berkeley.edu/article/item/what_makes_a_hero#thank-influence.

Index

kingdom of the world, 138
Kohr, Leopold, 155

labor, social division of, 32
lamb, significance of, 121
Larkin, Philip, 150
Lasch, Christopher, 159
law, 31, 139
Lee, Spike, 97
Leibnitzes, 49–50
Lewis, C. S., 158
life
    embrace of, 67
    pleasures of, 67
    worth of, 42–46, 54, 60, 61, 62
living death, 65–70
love
    abolishing law in favor of, 139
    fragility of, 31
    of God, 142
    Jesus and, 136–37
    limitations of, 31
    transformation of, 26
Lowell, James Russell, 118
Loyola, St. Ignatius, 109
Ludlum, Robert, 92

MacArthur, Douglas, 107
Macaulay, Thomas, 82
MacCulloch, Diarmaid, 91, 95, 99
magic, 68
Mahayana Buddhism, 83
Malcolm X, 96–97
Malta, 160
Marcus Aurelius, 48
Martha, 95
martyrdom, 53, 116–17n1
Marx, Karl, 139
Mary, 95
Masaccio, 124–25
Maslow, Abraham H., 73, 74
Masoretic text, 122n8
materialism, 56
Mawson, Tim, 73
maybes, 61
Mayle, Peter, 92
McCarthy, Joseph, 106

McCowen, Alec, 94
Mead, Margaret, 76
melancholy, 43, 49, 52
metaphysics
    appearances and, 28–29
    change and, 27
    intellectual alternatives in, 27–28
    as meta-humanity, 30
    overview of, 27
    as realism, 28
    regularities and, 29
    structure and, 29
Michelini, Daniel, 53
Michelini, Susanna, 53
midnight view, 47
military draft, 109
Milton, John, 115, 125
Mistler's Exit (Begley), 124–25
Moltmann, Jürgen, 123n9
moral exemplars, 77
morality, 39
moral philosophy, 35
moral theory, 34–35
Moriarty, John, 150, 151–52
Moses, 134
mountain climbing analogy, 60

Nagy, Gregory, 70–71
Nakamura, Jeanne, 74
naturalism, 56
natural science, 27, 29–30
natural theology, 48
nature, 50, 51, 55, 57–58, 157
neutrality, 57
Nietzsche, Friedrich, 69–70, 103, 119–20, 121, 133, 139
Nixon, Richard, 109
Northwestern University, 109

obligation, universalizing of, 36
One No, Many Yeses (Kingsworth), 145
Oppenheimer, Robert, 15
optimism, 47, 48, 61
Otto, Rudolph, 81

pain, 13, 16–17
Pantera, 93

Made in the USA
Monee, IL
22 September 2024

66332747R00105